THERE'S ALWAYS A WAY TO
SELL YOUR
BUSINESS

THERE'S ALWAYS A WAY TO
SELL YOUR BUSINESS

100 Tales from the Trenches by a Master Intermediary

DOUG ROBBINS

BPS
books

Published in 2010 by
BPS Books
Toronto and New York
bpsbooks.com
A division of Bastian Publishing Services Ltd.

ISBN 978-1-926645-24-7

Cataloguing in Publication Data available from Library and Archives Canada.

Cover design: Gnibel
Text design and typesetting: Daniel Crack, Kinetics Design, kdbooks.ca

Contents

Acknowledgments

I do a fair amount of public speaking – fifteen to thirty speeches a year. I always lace my speeches with tales to illustrate the points I want to make. In addition, I write many articles containing such tales.

So I thought writing this book would be a piece of cake. I assumed that with a concentrated effort it might take a week or ten days at the most. Given the many, many anecdotes at my disposal, I could just sit down, tell them to my dictating machine, upload them to my laptop, and then drag them into Word and print them. Done!

Little did I know that ten days would turn into almost eight hundred hours spanning more than two years. It turned out to be one HUGE piece of cake.

For their help and support during this lengthy process (and throughout my career), I wish to thank:

Marie, my wife of thirty-six years, for putting up with my "entrepreneurial weeks." Many times those weeks exceeded a hundred hours. There were a few times (not many) when I stood her up at a restaurant or left her standing at a function because I was tied up with a client.

My son, Mark, for his encouragement.

Joyce Hansen of Class Act Connections, our public relations company, for prodding and pushing me to get all these tales into some kind of a book.

My staff, for their patience and support. They put up with all my talk about the book and they spent a lot of time supporting me instead of doing some of the (more important) things they felt needed to be done.

Mary Ann Matthews, for making sense of all the tales and putting them into sequence.

Last but not least, I really must thank all of my customers and clients throughout the years. Without their activities and real-life experiences, I would have no tales to tell.

Introduction

There are over six million businesses in Canada and the United States. Over the next twenty-five years, a large majority of these businesses will close, merge, amalgamate, be taken public, go broke, or be sold.

The purpose of this book is not only to get owners to consider and review the process of selling their business but also to give them a view of some of the things that can go right ... or not so right.

Selling a business is one of the most important decisions in a business owner's life. It is filled with excitement and numerous other emotions, including fear, anxiety, and uncertainty about the future. In many cases these emotions can cause an owner to build a moat, or trench, around the castle of their business.

There are only two ways for owners to get out of the trench. One is to be pro-active, taking charge of the sale. Owners of this type take the appropriate steps to build a drawbridge so they can exit the business in an orderly and timely way.

The other is to be reactive. Owners who take this approach have to be helped out of the trench – or be hauled out in a box – because they have done little or nothing to make other choices available.

Neither option is easy.

The reasons for selling a business are as varied and as complex as the owners. Here are just of a few of the questions business owners ask:

- What will I do with myself after the business is sold?
- Will I get enough money from my business to retire safely?
- What is my business worth?
- What about my family? My kids?
- Will the new owner look after the employees?
- Will the new owner treat my customers as well as I have?
- How do I maintain confidentiality about the sale?
- How do I protect my intellectual property?
- How do I find the right buyer?

... and the list goes on and on.

The purpose of this book is to give you an insight into the complexities of selling your business as well as a sense of the elements you need to act on to achieve a timely sale at the best possible price. Helping business owners sell is what I do for a living – and it has been my privilege to do so for the past thirty-six years.

I believe the best way to learn is through stories. That's why this book, rather than containing lots of instructional verbiage about the process of selling a business, informs you through case studies, or rather, Tales from the Trenches. These are true stories of business owners. Many of them did not have a specific business plan or an exit strategy. Some of them did. (The names of owners and the names of their companies, along with their locations, have been altered to maintain confidentiality – and in some cases to avoid causing embarrassment.)

Each tale in this book is told to illustrate a point or emphasize an issue of importance. Each one illustrates the humanity and complexity of an individual involved in this life-altering decision. Each provides an answer to the abovementioned and many other often-asked questions ... in very human and unusual ways.

So I hope you will sit back and enjoy my tales. (There are many more to follow in subsequent books.) I believe you may find one or two that hit pretty close to your own experience.

Author's Note

When you sell your house, you put up a sign. Along comes someone who wants to buy your house. You sell it. Everyone signs the appropriate papers. A month or two later the moving truck shows up and off you go to your new home.

Selling a business is not like that at all. There are so many more variables. These make selling a business very complex. For example, a lot of people will be involved in selling your business. It's not just you and the buyer. Selling will include any or all of the following:

- **Accountant** – to make sure the transaction is structured properly and the taxes are calculated correctly.

- **Lawyer** – to write up the agreement and ensure that all the terms and conditions in that agreement comply with laws, rules, and regulations that relate to the business that is being sold. Your lawyer is on hand to handle tax requirements on any statute law. He or she also has to ensure that the buyer is secure; that his warranty representations are reasonable; and that any deferred payments, such as notes, etc., are likely to be paid. Your lawyer will look for security on promissory notes, mortgages, and management contracts.

- **Company Banker or Financial/Investment Advisor** – to ensure that you take the money you receive and place it in an income-generating portfolio that is secure and meets your criteria to sustain you through your retirement years.

- **Insurance Company** – to determine whether your life insurance policy should remain in your hands or in your children's hands and whether it needs to be restructured.

- **Employees** – to make sure your employees are cared for. This can be an important issue. I've had deals fall apart because the buyer wasn't going to treat the employees in a way that satisfied the seller. Other people don't care about their employees. If you care about your employees, then you have to ensure that your goals are not going to jeopardize them. They may inconvenience them a little bit, but not significantly.

- **Spouse** – to determine your family affairs. It may be that your wife or husband doesn't want you at home managing the kitchen. Many of my clients have sold their business and then come back saying, "My wife/husband kicked me out. I've got to get a job or go do something or get away."

- **Children** – to find out their personal and business goals. Most parents want their son or daughter to follow in their footsteps. That's only natural, but it's not always the reality. Everyone's different. Your kids may not want to work in your business.

- **Family** – to determine who is going to take the proceeds of this business and make sure they are invested properly.

- **Psychologist** – to help you ascertain how advisable it is for you to bring your children into the business. Psychology has reached a high level of accuracy in predicting failure.

All of a sudden a lot of people are going to be affected by your decisions. Ultimately you have to decide what is best for you, given your circumstances.

Most business owners decide to sell their business because they think that's all they can do. Not so. There are other options, as I make clear in chapter 26, Fourteen Alternatives to Selling. At least consider these options before making your final decision to sell.

This book is designed to illustrate the elements that impact a sale. If you get the sequence of these elements out of order, or overlook an element, the results of the sale may be far less than what you, as the business owner, anticipated. In some cases, the sale may never happen at all. (See the tale Causing a Landslide in chapter 5 and Crying over Spilled Oil in chapter 15.)

Time is such an important factor. It takes time to plan a business exit strategy. Surely you should spend more time planning your business exit than your next summer vacation. When planning a vacation, choices have to be made in advance: what places to visit, the means of transportation to get there, where to stay, which tours to take, where to eat, and so on. When planning a business exit, you need to consider such questions as:

- When do I sell?
- How do I structure the transaction?
- To whom do I sell?
- For how much?
- Why am I selling the business?
- What am I going to do after?
- How will I invest the proceeds?
- When do I call in my lawyer?

- When do I call in my accountant?
- What kind of a lawyer and accountant do I require?
- Should I have an advisory board?
- What about my family?
- How about my employees?
- What am I going to do with an extra sixty-eight hours per week?

As the tales that follow illustrate in detail, you need to know and understand all of these elements as you move ahead in your business to create your strategic exit plan. In a nutshell, the message of this book is:

– get a plan –

– take the time to sell your business properly –

the right way

at the right time

to the right buyer

for the right price

and the right terms and conditions

Chapter 1

I'm Going to Retire ... Maybe

Most business owners, when you ask them when
they are going to sell, will say, "Oh, in a few years."

1 **A CLIENT'S FAVOURITE NUMBER**
We recently asked a long-time client, "When are you
going to sell your business?"

"Oh in about five years," he said.

That has been his answer for a long time – I think it's safe
to say for twenty years. It's always in about five years. He has no
intentions of selling or retiring – he's just having too much fun
and making lots of money.

How old do you think he is?

Well, the last time we asked him the big question, he was
seventy-nine ...

> You really need to have a vision of where you want to
> be in your life. If you don't have a vision, you will probably
> miss a lot of life – in five-year chunks.
>
> You put a lot of blood, sweat, and tears into your
> own business. You continue to make a huge emotional
> and psychological investment in it. Your business is
> fascinating. Your business is challenging. It may well be
> a source of social networks and personal relationships.
> Many owners have a lot of fun with their business.

2 *It's Their Party ...*

Speaking of networks and relationships, I can relate to that.

When I left A&W Restaurants as their manager for Ontario, I oversaw a hundred stores. My role was to sell franchises and resell them for those who wanted to retire. So a lot of those fellows became my business friends. We looked forward to seeing one another a couple of times a year.

The company's annual three-day conference in Montreal was a few months after I left, which was in November 1974. Naturally, I wasn't invited. I felt glum, alone, rejected, isolated, and ostracized. I knew I didn't belong – I had quit – but I felt left out anyway.

Anticipating this reality is a major cause of procrastination among business owners. It's something for you to watch out for.

> Here's a tale about someone who did everything the way a businessperson ought to. He searched out competent advice when he wasn't sure. He surrounded himself with competent employees. He was always looking seven to ten years ahead.

3 *"Why Would I Want to Sell?"*

In 1983 we sold a business with sales of $750,000 to a marketing executive by the name of Tom.

Tom came back to us in 1990, having increased the company's sales to $3 million, and told us he was ready to sell.

Our Comprehensive Business Analysis revealed a very bright future for his product and business.

We strongly urged Tom to create an advisory board and to do some in-depth research on equipment and his markets, particularly in the United States. He and his advisors then completed a business plan. It indicated to him that the future was indeed quite bright if he changed direction.

Tom returned in 1996 with sales of $7 million.

"I am now ready to sell my business," he said.

After we completed a Comprehensive Business Analysis, I asked him, "Tom, when was the last time you had a complete physical examination?"

He looked at me strangely.

"Why do you ask?"

"At your age of sixty, I don't want to encourage you to keep the business if your health is weakening."

About four weeks later Tom called me.

"My health is very good," he said. "Now, when can we get together so you can tell me the results of what you've learned about my business?"

"The results show that there has been a significant shift in the marketplace for your product lines," I said. "New technology is now available that will make you even more productive and allow you to enter a new market."

Again he decided to keep his business.

I called Tom in 2006.

"Perhaps it's time for us to sit down and talk about you selling your business," I said.

After all, he was now seventy years old.

"Perhaps you should now start the process to put your affairs in order," I added.

There was a long pause.

"I don't think you understand," Tom finally said. "I followed all the advice that you've given along the years and the advice of my advisors. I have surrounded myself with good people. I now work only six hours a day and work only three days a week. And I'm in the office for only one of those three days. And furthermore, I now take six months of vacation every year.

My sales are $18 million and I keep almost $2 million. Why would I want to sell my business?"

He went on to say how much he appreciated the help I had given him over the years and that he wanted me to know I was named in his will.

I became quite excited when I heard that. Then Tom explained that his will instructed his executor to call our firm to sell the business when he passed on.

Chapter **2**

A Vision of Tomorrow

Some people get hung up on the question, "Why would I want to give up my business when there's no certainty what life will look like tomorrow?"

Without that clear vision, you're likely to want to keep the status quo and carry on with your business. It is hard to move forward and get past that huge barrier called CHANGE.

Having your own business is like giving birth to a child. You watch it grow. You become emotionally involved. You invest a lot of time in it. The idea of selling it and stopping all of your activity is difficult.

Then certain circumstances make selling a crisis.

Those circumstances may be one or several of the following:

- a serious health issue for you, a close friend, or family member
- the untimely death of a family member or close friend
- technology overtaking your company's methods
- a key employee leaves to start their own business or goes to work for a competitor
- the business deteriorates as you age and can't do as much as you used to
- the effects of age. (You may find yourself asking,

"Who was that potential large customer I met last week? What was his name?")

When the crisis hits, selling the business becomes a reaction rather than a carefully planned action.

4 READING THE RIOT ACT

We brought in an offer that was above the expectations of our clients, Mabel and Fred. They owned a party rental business, renting party tents, tables, chairs, carpets, dance floors, dishes, coffee urns, chocolate fountains, champagne fountains, crystal glassware, wine glasses, tablecloths, napkins, and costumes.

Mabel was sixty-nine years old. She was probably eighty to ninety pounds overweight and had difficulty moving. Most of the running around was done by Fred, her seventy-six-year-old husband.

Mabel took a look at the offer and suddenly decided she wasn't going to sell. She still felt pretty good, she said. She enjoyed coming to work every day.

"And if I did sell, what on earth would I do with all my time?" she asked.

I finally had to read her the riot act.

"Look, Mabel," I said, "our contract says that if we get this amount of money or more for you, you have to pay us our commission. You don't have to sell, but now you have to get out your chequebook."

That was pretty drastic. I didn't want to take this approach, but I suspected it was the only way to get through to her.

Mabel went away and thought about it. After careful consideration, she decided to proceed with the sale. This was in her best interest, because Fred was no longer able to maintain the pace he had established years earlier. He was falling farther and farther behind as the business continued to grow.

Mabel was really a working manager as opposed to a managing manager. She was not current with today's business standards. In fact, she was still using the One-Write accounting system and maintaining inventory on a card system. The pace of business had changed and she couldn't relate.

My shock tactic was the best way to show Mabel that she really had no alternative but to sell.

> Like Mabel and many other business owners, you may not have a clear vision of tomorrow. Like Mabel, you may be reacting to your perceived emptiness of what tomorrow will bring.
>
> "What will I do if I don't go to work?" you may ask.
>
> Creating that opportunity, creating that vision of tomorrow, finding out your options, will make the transition much easier for you.

5 HITTING THE GOLF LINKS

I took the time to help Mabel visualize what life could be like without the business.

"Mabel, there are so many things out there that you can do," I said. "Time with your children, and more importantly, your grandchildren. And what about renewing acquaintances and spending some time with friends? You can participate in community activities."

I added that her business skills could come in handy, too.

"You can use them to sit on boards or committees of various organizations like the Chamber of Commerce, hospital boards, United Way, YWCA. You will now have more time to spend with your church. Hey, and what about playing golf?"

It turned out that golf was something Mabel had always wanted to do.

I made a point of staying in touch with Mabel and Fred.

I occasionally dropped in when passing by and our friendship grew. I always received (and sent) a Christmas card. I also attended the christening of a new grandchild and Fred's funeral.

Mabel went on to become an avid golfer. She often complained that she didn't have enough time to do everything she wanted.

The day after you sell your business you are going to be just as intelligent as you were the day before you sold. You are going to have just as much energy. And you will have just as much creativity and just as much motivation.

What you won't have – at least not at first blush – is something to do. You will now have sixty or more unstructured waking hours per week that you didn't have before. These will no longer be filled up with your business.

If you have nothing to do to fill those hours and utilize your intelligence, motivation, and creativity, life probably will not be nearly as enjoyable.

6 Visions

Paul came to see us when his business had become too demanding given his serious back problems. Quite frankly, he couldn't carry on any more and he was only forty-four. He was pretty negative. He had to sell his business and he didn't want to.

We asked him what he was going to do. He didn't have a clue. We suggested other careers that were related to his business. He was young, sharp, and willing to learn. He quickly realized there were lots of things he could do that didn't require physical activity.

He walked away feeling really positive about the future.

All we did was help him fill in his vision of tomorrow. Now he was actually looking forward to selling his business.

Everyone needs a vision of tomorrow. Planning life after exiting a business is just as important as developing a strategic exit strategy.

As we grow older, it takes us longer to do the things we did in our youth. We don't have the energy or the stamina we did in our twenties or thirties. Our interests have evolved but we may not realize that things have changed. Chances are we don't go to rock concerts anymore, but we may attend local theatre. Taking the time to understand what we now enjoy doing, and then planning to do it, is an extremely important part of selling our business.

I like to suggest to our clients that we negotiate a management-consulting contract for them with the new owner of their business for five years: three months full time, three months part time, and four and a half years as an occasional consultant. (This is a great tax-planning strategy.) The seller is thus faced with a gradual but defined change in activity from business to life after business.

7 No Time to Age

A lot of business owners contribute their know-how to service clubs. So do some retired guys who have run successful businesses. These good souls have been involved at a high level in business and now work with United Way or Goodwill or sit on the hospital board or the school board.

I sat on the board of governors of the local college. One of the chaps on the board – he's now an emeritus governor – was a doctor who had been a teaching doctor. This man has travelled the world since he retired. He has been to Africa, India, and China to set up foundations. He has supervised numerous projects for Rotary International.

He is busier now than when he was practicing. He's so fulfilled and he's well into his eighties.

Another chap I bumped into yesterday, also a member of a Rotary club, is in the insurance business. Bob is more than ninety years old, but you'd swear he's is not a day over seventy. He's busy every day, out of his house at six-thirty a.m., returning at six-thirty p.m., six days a week. He is just go-go-go-go-go. And you know what? He hasn't had time to get old.

I think there's a lot of truth in that. Business owners worry that they'll grow old if they quit. The secret is, *sell your business, but don't slow down.*

Chapter 3

How to Fill Those Sixty Hours

Selling the business isn't an end. It's a beginning. But the beginning of what?

If business owners fail to see what's out there for them if they sell, they will prefer to stay in that protective trench of their business. As mentioned in the previous chapter, it's important for such owners to have a clear vision of their future.

There is a general and unspoken fear out there that if you don't have something to do after you retire you will be dead in three years. We have heard that statistic many times. People work all their lives to get their pension when they turn sixty-five. And then they're dead at age sixty-eight or sixty-nine.

To leave work after thirty-five or forty years may sound like a great idea. You may be ready for it. But when you begin to consider the reality of what it will be like after retirement, the uncertainty can be pretty intimidating. If you haven't planned, you may be dragging your heels. Fear of the unknown is a powerful disincentive.

Here's a tale about a savvy entrepreneur who understood the value of making the transition and filling in those sixty working hours in a very practical way.

8 JUST ANOTHER DAY AT THE OFFICE

When Charlie was seventy-three, he sold his company, which was housed in a 150,000-square-foot building that he also owned. His sales were about $30 million a year. He told the buyer he would sell his building and his business only if they let him use a corner office for as long as he wanted. In addition, he needed somebody to answer his phone. The buyers thought this was a small price to pay and didn't really object to his request.

Every day Charlie went to the office. He read the newspapers. His buddies came to the office to visit and they would go out for lunch. His secretary answered his phone calls and gave him his messages. She even got him the occasional cup of coffee. He remained quite active in Rotary, sitting on several committees.

Charlie didn't give up the part of his life he recognized as being essential. He said he kept that essential part by going to work every day. He also said his wife would kill him if he tried to manage the house.

Charlie lived for fifteen years after that.

As much as owners say, "Oh yeah, I want to sell my business," there may be another part of them saying, "Oh my gosh, I don't want to sell my business. What will I do with myself with all that extra time on my hands?"

As mentioned, those two to three years after retirement – whether retirement happens at sixty-two, sixty-five, sixty-eight, or seventy-two – are critical in terms of longevity. Some people don't make it. Retiring and adapting to new circumstances can play a significant role in people's lives.

Tragically, some will not have the opportunity to make that decision about retirement. It is taken out of their hands by sudden illness or unforeseen circumstances.

In these cases, it is left to a family member or partner to carry on.

9 Her Cheque Will Be in the Mail

A number of years ago, a banker referred me to a widow named Bettina. Her husband, Samji, had created a high-tech business and had died quite unexpectedly. Sales were about $1.2 million, with a profit of about $100,000.

Bettina inherited the business. Over the course of the next seven or eight months, she found she was unable to operate it effectively. The company began to lose money. Her banker, her lawyer, and her accountant recommended that she close and liquidate the business. But Bettina felt that the technology that Samji had invented and patented was of value.

When we met with Bettina, we discussed the current operating situation and provided some advice on how we could reduce some of the costs and thereby reduce some of the losses.

"It's probably going to take four to six months to find a buyer and two to three months to close the transaction after we find a buyer for you," I said. "Are you up to the challenge?"

Bettina went away and thought about it. A couple of days later she came back.

"Yes," she said, "I'm up to the challenge and ready to go."

So we got to work. Three months later we found a buyer and convinced him to purchase the fixed assets of the business and the inventory. He was also to pay a royalty on sales for the next fifteen years.

Bettina collected the accounts receivable; retained the little bit of cash that was in the company; discharged the accounts payable and a small operating line of credit; and wound up on the positive side of the ledger.

Plus she had those royalty payments to look forward to.

10 No Substitute for Experience

I received a visit from a young lady inquiring about the process of selling her husband's business. He had passed away suddenly from a heart attack at forty years of age, leaving her with two small children to care for. The business was a small metalworking company employing twelve.

"Is there anyone in the business who could operate it?" I asked.

"There's no one else. Just me," Nancy replied. "I've been running it for about four months now. After Eddy died, I decided it couldn't be all that hard to run. So I left my job to take on this responsibility."

Nancy had some basic bookkeeping skills, excellent communication skills, and a little knowledge about the business itself from her husband. She did not have a good understanding of accounting or the intricacies of the day-to-day operation of the company.

"I'm really enjoying the challenge of operating this business," she said. "But sometimes I find the employees difficult to manage. I'm also having problems with some of the quoting and pricing of services and products. It's kind of stressful."

The stress is what tipped the balance and convinced her to ask about the process of selling the business.

She heard us out but decided to keep the business and operate it herself.

Nancy came back about a year later. Running a business was definitely not what she wanted to do with the rest of her life, she told us. She was ready to sell.

Our phase one process turned up some irregularities in her company's accounting procedures. Further investigation showed the company was not making the money reported on the books. The accountant quickly revised the statements. Now we had a business for sale that was not profitable. The company had taken a turn for the worse and was losing about $20,000 per month.

A turnaround team was sent in. They quickly uncovered an error in the quoting program and implemented a number of changes. Within a few months the business was profitable once again.

Four months later the business was sold to a father and son team who had a lifetime of experience operating this type of business.

In spite of the complexity, in spite of the difficulties, in spite of some of the stresses, entrepreneurs genuinely enjoy a large part of what they do. If you're like many entrepreneurs, you say you don't go to work, you go to play, because you genuinely enjoy your business.

"Why should I stop playing?" you say. "My business is like a hobby for me."

Some of an entrepreneur's enjoyment comes from interactions with people. Some of it comes from the challenge of solving problems. Some of it comes from creativity or from succeeding or helping other people to succeed.

As athletes age, their bodies no longer perform as well. They just can't do it any more. It's clear to them that they have to retire. But an entrepreneur can enjoy his business and continue in it until … Or could it be that they just don't notice that they can't do it any more?

Older entrepreneurs have experience. They have gone through thousands of situations, and that gives them greater decision-making skills. Newcomers don't have that depth of experience to draw on, but they do have more energy and stamina.

There's a point where the two lines cross but rare is the entrepreneur who recognizes when that happens.

As my accountant often says, "They remember how fast they could run as a boy as they hobble along with their cane."

Chapter *4*

What's My Business Worth?

Most small to medium-sized businesses are privately owned and operated by an entrepreneur who is busy keeping track of the day-to-day affairs of the business. Usually overworked, sometimes careless or lazy, such entrepreneurs rarely have a long-term plan for the future of their company. As a result, they may fail to recognize opportunities that are standing there right at their front door.

Often a slight shift in focus can produce a significant increase in the value of the company.

11 MAKING IT WORTHWHILE

A decade ago I gave a workshop in a small northeastern community. As a result, our firm was retained by a small business doing sales of approximately $1 million. They wanted an assessment of their company.

We did our phase one Comprehensive Analysis, looking at the operating procedures within the business and at the people, too.

We reported to the owners, Joe and Sarah, that their business was worth $250,000.

Joe got pretty upset.

"Hey, you guys don't know what you're talking about. My business is worth at least a million."

We walked Joe through five evaluation methods to show him why the business was not worth that much.

I looked Joe straight in the eye.

"You would like $1 million for your company, right?" I asked him.

"Yes!"

"Then the first thing you need to do is get your lazy ass out of bed every morning and get to work before your employees do. No more of this arriving at nine-thirty or ten a.m."

I definitely had Joe's attention.

"Second, bring in a bag lunch and eat with your employees. No more two-hour lunches."

Smoke was starting to come out of his ears.

"Third, you will be the last one to leave the business at the end of the day, after all your employees go home. And fourth, you will work diligently every day.

"If you do that for a couple of years, this business will start to make real money. Your customers and employees will have more respect for your firm and the profit will be there to justify the value you are looking for. The sales will grow."

Four years later one of my salesmen came to me and said, "Joe wants to know if you are still angry with him."

"I never *was* angry with him. I just told it the way it was."

I got Joe on the phone and after a few opening pleasantries, he said, "If I send you my statements for the last couple of years, would you take a quick look and see if perhaps we should be talking about selling?"

He did and we did.

The business sold about six months later for $980,000.

An intermediary can look at a business and see opportunities the owner may not see. Doing some things a little differently may be all it takes to increase the value of the business. It may be changing the marketing strategy, investing differently in capital equipment, and/or expanding the territory.

12 THINKING OUTSIDE THE WAREHOUSE

I had a client who was in the business of manufacturing furniture. Troy had a number of large customers. He manufactured some products on an exclusive basis to some of them.

The company's rented warehouse was 25,000 square feet, twenty-five-feet high, and filled with $1.5 million worth of finished goods.

The warehouse cost approximately $80,000 a year in rent. On top of that there were real estate taxes, utility bills, and guard service costs, for a total bill of about $125,000 a year.

Troy had been renting the warehouse for two years, incurring expenses of $250,000, and the furniture in it hadn't moved during that period of time.

"Troy, what's the problem here?" I asked.

"Well, the furniture was designed by our largest customer and we made it anticipating orders that never came. We want to keep this customer, so we've got to look after his furniture."

"By getting rid of this warehouse and all this furniture, two things are going to happen," I said. "First of all, you can save your company $125,000 a year on rent and related costs and you can save interest on the $1.5 million tied up in inventory. With that inventory converted to cash, your company will become flush again."

"I don't know," he replied. "I don't want to upset Herman. He's my major customer. He buys about $2 million of product from me a year."

I got Troy's permission to meet with Herman directly and off I went.

I explained to Herman that Troy had all this product of his and I wanted Herman to take it and sell it.

"No, we don't want to take it," Herman said. "There's no way we can sell it."

"Okay, then we want the opportunity to sell it ourselves."

Herman and his people hemmed and hawed and said, "We don't really want you to do that. That furniture has our brand on it."

"Well, you've got to do one of two things. You either buy it or we'll sell it. You see, if this product isn't moved, you may no longer have a supplier."

This elicited more hemming and hawing.

Knowing that Herman's company had a number of retail outlets throughout Canada, I came up with an idea.

"Herman, pick six retail outlets, preferably in large shopping centres, and have a truck clearance sale. Our client will bring in three tractor-trailers to each of these six locations, filled with inventory. We can sell the furniture right off the back of the trucks and we'll replace the trailers as they become empty. Put some scaffolding up at the end of the trailers to make a bit of a show area, and run those sales very aggressively for four weeks."

After much thought and prolonged negotiations, Herman agreed.

Our client, Troy, contributed $100,000 for advertising. He reduced the price of the total inventory to $1.25 million. The furniture was sold at half price (retail). Six weeks later the entire inventory was gone.

Herman's company made a significant profit for itself. Troy cleared a warehouse and freed up $1.115 million in cash that was tied up in inventory. He reduced his annual operating expenses by almost $200,000 (in warehouse costs and interest saved).

Many times the value of the assets is worth more than the value of the business, as in the following case.

13 HOLLYWOOD ENDING

Many years ago Pat met with us about selling his drive-in movie theatre. The theatre was doing about $1 million. Pat was making about $100,000 – the extent of the theatre's profit. The business was worth between $500,000 and $600,000.

The drive-in was located on ten acres of land in the middle of the city. If you remember, these theatres in times of old were built on farmland on the outskirts of cities. Well, in this case, the city had expanded and now enveloped the theatre. The land the theatre was on was worth many times more than the value of the business.

We recommended that the client simply find a good commercial real estate broker and put a housing development on it.

Pat retired a multi-millionaire.

Sometimes it's necessary to take one step backward in order to take two steps forward. Here's a tale with a most unusual outcome.

14 TROUBLE IN A BUNKER

Approximately fifteen years ago I received a call from a cranky individual named Ben. He said he had heard me talk at a Rotary meeting a year earlier and wanted to know if I was still in business.

"Yes sir," I said. "I have been here for eighteen years and am trying to be for another eighteen."

"Well, you better get over here and see me," Ben said.

The following day, I visited his plant. A fascinating facility, operating out of 140,000 square feet on fifteen acres of well-manicured land in a flood plain of a major river. The building was approximately forty years old and was in good shape.

I sat down with Ben and reviewed his operation. I noted that his sales, at $12 million, were not that high for the size of the facility. We talked about his business, his problems, his challenges, and our process.

Ben reluctantly agreed to spend the money to have a phase one Comprehensive Business Analysis completed.

As we went through the facility, we noticed that a division of the company was being operated by his son. This division had no compatibility with the main operation and really ought not to have been there.

I explained to Ben that a number of things really needed to be done. One of them was a phase one Environmental Impact Study. A building this old, particularly since it was on a flood plain, needed to have a clean bill of health before we took the business to market. Once again, he reluctantly agreed, and we hired an engineering firm to do the work.

I suggested to Ben that we needed to separate his son's business from the company. I encouraged him to put it into a separate corporation owned by his son. We would do this in a tax-favourable way, but the process would take two years in order to "crystallize" and avoid extra income taxes on the sale of Ben's business after the restructuring.

One of the employees of the environmental engineering company came back and said, "We believe we have a major problem in Bunker C."

Bunker C oil was used to heat the plant. The problem was that the underground tanks in that bunker were next to a huge concrete pad on which sat all of the transformers for the company's operations. There was a broken seam where the steam generator was attached to one of the underground tanks. As a result, Bunker C oil had leaked out around the tank and underneath this hydro pad.

Furthermore, the pad was in a flood zone. The problem had to be fixed before we went to market.

This meant the plant would have to be shut down for two weeks. The transformers would have to be disconnected and moved off the pad. The pads would have to be torn up while the spill was cleaned up. New concrete pads would have to be poured before the transformers could be reinstalled. The clean-up was postponed until the plant shut down for summer vacation.

I said to Ben, "While we clean up out back and wait for the restructuring to crystallize, we ought to look at some value enhancement opportunities. We should also take a long, hard look at the process and products you're making and the customers you're selling these products to."

Our research department identified thirty other potential customers that he and his sales manager could call on. Ben and his sales manager took this project seriously. Within twelve months they had landed $4 million worth of repeat annual business.

Now Ben's sales were $16 million. The value of the business went up substantially. The cost of the environmental clean-up was covered by the extra profits generated from the new customers over the following year.

We sold that business about thirty months later, for almost twice the amount at which it had been originally valued. (Note that a company's profits are usually made on the last 20% of revenue. If revenue is increased by an additional 20 to 25%, the profits will double – which results in a doubling of the value of the business.)

Chapter *5*

Shh – Keep It Quiet

Confidentiality is one of the most important things for an owner to consider when it's time to sell. In fact, as our experience has shown us time and time again, sellers who maintain a very high level of confidentiality are much more likely to get a favourable amount for their company.

If you have been approached by a buyer and you decide to sell the business without professional assistance, you must have the buyer sign a Confidentiality/Non-Interference Agreement. If the buyer provides one (and often they do), have your lawyer or an intermediary review it with you. Many so-called buyers are simply competitors looking to acquire information through industrial espionage. A business intermediary or a good transaction lawyer can provide you with an agreement that will protect your long-term interests.

15 SHE GOT HER NAME IN THE PAPER
Martha decided it was time to sell her small shop, The Flower Garden. She ran ads in the local newspaper looking for someone to buy the business. In a very short time her intentions became general knowledge in the community.

As a result, her two key employees promptly quit and went to work for another company, creating operating problems – and great stress – for Martha.

The rumour mill started to grind. Suppliers became nervous, losing confidence in Martha's continued ability to pay bills on time. A major customer who spent about $800 per week went to a competitor, thereby reducing her profits and the overall value of her business.

Had she used a professional business intermediary, that newspaper ad would never have been run. Martha could have continued to run her business profitably while getting into position to sell her company.

It is critical for you to keep news of a pending sale away from the employees. Employees have a variety of reactions when they hear about a sale.

Some will be concerned about the security of their job and about their mortgage and car payments.

Others will leave the company and go to work for a competitor.

Still others will come back and demand a raise because they may, correctly or incorrectly, believe the company just cannot get by without them.

Some will get over this concern and realize that the business, if sold, will still require their services as employees.

But all of this anxiety and stress can be avoided simply by keeping notice of the sale confidential.

16 CAUSING A LANDSLIDE

I sold Landslide Towing a number of years ago. The company had ten vehicles: six of them were owned by independent drivers and four of them were owned by the company. Landslide had central dispatch, a contract with the local police department, a secure compound, and a good reputation in the community.

Landslide was being sold to a competitor in the next community, which made it a good fit from both a strategic operation and a marketing perspective. The merged companies would result in substantial operational savings to the new owner. The buyer was paying a significant premium for the business.

Jim, Landslide's seller, was a bit nervous about the sale. In addition, he was a very talkative guy.

The transaction was scheduled to close on December 31. I called Jim virtually every day that month and said, "You haven't told anybody yet, have you?"

"No, sir. I haven't told a soul," was always his answer.

When I called on the 23rd, Jim said, "I think I may have done a bad thing."

"What did you do?"

"Well, we had our staff Christmas party last night and I had a few drinks more than I should have had and became rather emotional. I said, 'I'm going to miss you guys.' They immediately wanted to know what I meant by that. I had to tell them that I had sold the business to Al in the next community."

"What happened after that?"

"Not much. Everything was fairly quiet and we all shook hands and went home. Do you think I screwed up my deal?"

"I don't know. Only time will tell."

On the 27th, those six independent truck drivers got together, went down to a registry office in Toronto, and incorporated a new company. The next day they were in business and in competition with our client.

Jim's transaction never closed.

The best way to deal with the issues surrounding confidentiality is to take every precaution to ensure that nobody, but nobody, finds out the business is for sale.

But how do you sell a business if nobody knows it is for sale?

The first thing to do is decide who needs to know and swear them to secrecy.

This will include your lawyer and accountant. Make sure their secretaries and partners are kept in the dark as long as possible. When they must be advised, tell them they must not discuss the file outside the office.

Many breaches of confidentiality have occurred in restaurants over lunch.

17 AN ILLIQUID LUNCH

A buyer, Frank, came to our office with his lawyer and accountant. He was looking to acquire a business that we had been discussing with him for a number of weeks. We talked over the file, discussing various aspects of the business.

Frank and his colleagues indicated that they would be prepared to deliver an offer to us within the next couple of days. They left our office at eleven-thirty a.m.

At approximately three-thirty that afternoon, we received a call from Bill, someone unknown to us. He said he had been in a restaurant for lunch and overheard three business guys talking about buying a business. He heard our company name and wanted to inquire about buying that business.

He came to our office the next morning and signed our Confidentiality/Non-Interference Agreement. He reviewed the business and put in an offer.

Bill happened to have been sitting in the booth next to Frank and his colleagues. He had overhead the exuberant and enthusiastic conversation about the business that Frank was about to buy and how he was going to buy it and what the offers were going to be and what the terms and conditions were going to be, and what the future potential of the business was and how he was going to take it to the next level.

Unfortunately for Frank, Bill was a competitor who knew all about the type of business under discussion. His own business was a synergistic and strategic fit with our client. Frank lost out because he couldn't keep his mouth shut.

Besides your lawyer and accountant, obviously your spouse will need to know. Emphasize with family the damage that can occur to the family's net worth if news of a pending sale were to get out. Never tell your banker what you are contemplating without having him sign a Confidentiality Agreement first.

Over the years, most of the breaches of confidentiality I have seen have occurred from one of these three sources: family, bankers, or trusted professionals.

The breaches are usually without malicious intent – they are just an accident or a slip of the tongue. But malicious or not, they can have a devastating effect.

18 LOSING LEVERAGE

A number of years ago, a small engineering firm was going through difficult times and as a result did not have the resources to give raises or pay bonuses.

Kevin, one of the senior employees, offered to take a small deferral in his pay until things got better, in exchange for a "few shares" in the company. Charlie, the owner, who was somewhat stressed by the current tight situation, was overcome with gratitude at Kevin's kind offer and agreed to give him 10% of the company.

Fast-forward eight years. Charlie was approached by one of his largest customers who wanted to buy the engineering firm. The timing was right for Charlie, who was now in his early sixties. He agreed to the sale.

One of the conditions of the sale was that Kevin had to sell his shares and, more importantly, sign an employment agreement.

That agreement was quite generous, offering Kevin a 35% wage increase over current market value for his skills.

However, Kevin learned through a breach in confidentiality by one of the buyer's employees that the buyer would not complete the transaction unless Kevin stayed. Kevin then demanded 50% of sale proceeds or he would not accept a job with the buyer.

Kevin went so far as to locate another job (at market value, I might add). He held out for the extra money for his shares.

The transaction was put on hold while discussions ensued with Kevin. He finally settled for 30% of the sales proceeds and the transaction was completed five months later than it would have otherwise. Legal, accounting, and other professional fees were three times higher than they would have been had confidence been kept.

Fortunately for Charlie, the purchaser agreed to pay a "little bit more" because of the breach in confidentiality.

It seems that no one is immune when it comes to confidentiality. I often say to financiers, "Are you going to finance this guy? Good. Then you need to sign a Confidentiality Agreement."

Here's a tale that illustrates why I make this request.

19 WHEN YOU LEAST EXPECT IT

I sold a business years ago in Oakville, Ontario, to a chap who had to go to his bank for financing. Our client, Dennis, used the MajorMinor Bank. It turned out that the purchaser, Alvin, used the same bank.

So the MajorMinor Bank manager of one branch called the MajorMinor Bank manager of the other branch.

"I see that Alvin is looking to buy Dennis' business," he said. "Tell me about the business."

And they chatted back and forth.

Dennis' bank manager called Dennis' office and said to his bookkeeper, "I see the business has been sold."

The bookkeeper didn't even know it had been put up for sale.

The moral of the story is that breaches in confidentiality can come from unexpected quarters. You would like to think that professionalism would prevail in these cases, but sadly that is often not the case.

The purchaser's request for financing had been turned down and the transaction never closed. The bookkeeper subsequently left, but fortunately none of the key employees did.

Note that in this case *both* bank managers had breached confidentiality.

Chapter 6

Bankers

It is important to understand the nature of a bank: how it works; how to interact with it; and what you can reasonably expect from it.

A bank makes money in two distinct ways: one is through service charges and the various fees charged for banking services; the second is by lending their depositors' money to people and charging higher interest than they pay for the deposits. When lending money, they are concerned with two things: security for the loan and cash flow.

Having now stated the obvious, we must remember that the bank is a service organization made up of lots of people. The key words here are "lots of people." This is a relationship business. You need to develop a trusting relationship with your banker; know and understand what the bank can do and cannot do; understand clearly what they expect from you; and know what you can expect from them.

Pretty simple when you think about it. So it should be, but I come back to the words "lots of people."

A group of people can look at the same thing and see or understand it differently from each other. Perceptions may differ. Communications may not be as clear as they should be. People may "understand" something that was not said or meant.

The following tales should give you a new view of bankers in general and your relationship with your bank in particular. I hope these tales will also give you an insight into the human side of banking.

Bankers can be your best friend or your biggest albatross.

20 SHOW ME THE MONEY

Corptech was a small manufacturer of electronic circuitry. Located some distance north of Toronto, it was a division of a large international conglomerate that no longer fit within the conglomerate's mandate. Sal, the purchaser, was a young engineer from Toronto who felt he could take this business to the next level.

The closing was being completed in Toronto. Financing had been arranged by one of the banks and the transaction was closing in Sal's lawyer's office. The banker was to appear in the lawyer's office at the appropriate time and bring a bank draft for the amount of money that had been arranged by Sal to close the transaction.

But the banker arrived without the money.

"Oh, I didn't realize I was supposed to have the money," he said.

He called over to his branch and said, "I need a draft for $1,750,000. Please have someone walk it over right away."

This was at two p.m.

It finally did arrive at four-thirty that afternoon and the transaction closed at about five-fifteen.

Eventually I got a chance to discuss this with the banker. It turns out that he had never been to a closing of a midsized business transaction before and thought the invitation to come over was a courtesy.

We look up to our bankers. We hold them in high esteem. Sometimes we even regard them with awe, because they control the money. But at the end of the day, they are just average guys.

21 WRONG TURN

We sold a printing business a few years ago to Gene. The transaction was to close on Thursday, November 10. Everything was going according to plan, except that the lawyers were running behind. The actual closing was to be completed in the boardroom of the purchaser's bank. The bank was providing the money to finally close the deal, so it made sense to go to Gene's bank to complete the transaction.

Gene's lawyer called the banker and said he was running "a few minutes" late. Instead of arriving at three p.m. he would likely be there at four and was that okay?

"That's just fine," the banker said. "I will be happy to wait for you."

Well, lawyers being lawyers, four really worked out to be four-thirty by the time we all finally arrived at the bank. The bank was about to close its doors. We went into the boardroom, shook hands with the banker, and completed the transaction with John, the seller. We were done by five-fifteen.

John's lawyer looked at the banker and said, "Okay, can we have the money?"

The banker looked at him and said, "What money?"

"The money your customer is borrowing to complete this transaction."

The banker said, "I didn't realize I was supposed to provide the money today. Nobody told me. I didn't order it."

The only reason we had gone to the bank was because that was where the money was. So all of a sudden it's past five and the bank is closed. The banker is being very congenial and nice by letting us use his boardroom.

Gene and John's lawyers looked at the banker and said, "Why do you think we came here?"

"Well, I wasn't sure of that. I thought you wanted to see our new boardroom."

In any event the transaction closed in escrow. The banker promised to wire the money right away. However, on November 11, Remembrance Day, all Canadian banks are closed. The earliest possible day to wire the money was first thing Monday morning.

John's lawyer said to the banker, "What happens to the money if Gene gets run over by a truck between now and Monday morning?"

"I haven't got a clue."

John's lawyer, feeling quite uncomfortable, said, "Tell you what. We'll arrange for Robbins to pick up the money first thing Monday morning."

"That's fine, but it's not necessary. I can have it wired to your account by nine-fifteen a.m."

By now the lawyer was getting quite agitated.

"No. I want Robbins to pick up the money."

The following day, I thought to myself, "Why do I want to drive forty miles to pick up the money; drive another sixty miles to deliver it; and then turn around and drive back home again – another hundred miles? That's a lot of driving to appease a lawyer because the banker misunderstood."

So I called Jack, a young MBA who had recently joined our firm, and said, "I would like you to go and run this errand for me on Monday. Be at this bank at nine a.m. sharp and call me as soon as you pick up the funds. Then I want you to deliver the cheque to the lawyer who is about sixty miles farther north."

At five minutes after nine on Monday morning, Jack called and said, "I have the funds and I'm on my way."

At ten-thirty a.m. I received a call from John's lawyer.

"What are you doing in your office?" he asked. "I thought you were supposed to pick up the money!"

"I sent Jack to pick it up and he should be there by now."

A long silence ensued. "He's not here."

At eleven a.m. John's lawyer called again. Still no Jack.

Same story at eleven-thirty.

At noon I got a call from Jack.

"I made a wrong turn on the highway and I realize that I am now about two hundred miles away from the seller's lawyer's offices."

The cheque was finally delivered at four that afternoon.

In spite of all the clichés that we hear about banks lending money as an umbrella and wanting the umbrella back when it rains, there are many great success stories about how bankers can help a businessperson.

For example, they can help owners make a quick solution.

22 A Second Chance

A number of years ago, Brian, about forty-eight years old, arrived at our offices unannounced. It was on a Thursday morning, at about nine-forty-five. He told us he wanted to sell his business. He came prepared with brochures, financial statements, the lease on his building, and lists of his equipment and employees.

Everything seemed in order.

It was a nice little business, doing about $1.2 million in revenue, showing a reasonable profit. There was no bank debt;

accounts payable only thirty-five days old; accounts receivable had been properly aged an average of forty-five days.

Brian signed a Listing Agreement and then inquired if he could have the money from the sale by noon on Friday, the following day. We asked why noon on Friday and he said he needed the money to meet payroll for Friday at four p.m.

I then asked the obvious question.

"Brian, if you could meet payroll tomorrow, would you still want to sell the business?"

"No way."

He had tried to collect his receivables early without success. He had used all of the company's free cash and his life savings and could see no way to meet payroll other than a quick sale of the business.

I called a young, enthusiastic bank manager at the local bank and asked him if he could spare half an hour … now. He came right over and arranged an operating line of credit. We tore up the Listing Agreement.

Brian came to see me about fifteen years later. We sold his business, then doing $2.5 million in revenue, and helped him retire.

Chapter *7*

Accountants

Accountants are a very competent bunch of people. For the most part, they deal with black-and-white issues. You know, one and one equals two – always has been and always will be. Some issues, like taxes, do provide colour and complexity. But most accountants know when they're outside their area of competence in tax and bring in other accountants who specialize in that area.

That said, there are certain exceptions to our accounting friends. It pays to be careful when you're working with one of them.

In my early years, I dealt mostly with very small businesses. Most of our buyers did not have an accountant so I had to refer them to one. After all, along with a lawyer, an accountant must be consulted before a business owner or buyer completes a transaction.

It is important to ensure that a buyer always has both an accountant and a lawyer and has consulted them before they enter into any kind of a binding agreement.

23 SELLER BEWARE
Early in my career I sent a number of buyers over to a particular accounting firm. But I couldn't understand why I was finding it difficult to get reasonable offers from those buyers in terms of the value of the business. As I explored the

situation further, I found that the accountants were telling them that they should be looking to pay only three to three and a half times profit for the business.

About six months after I made this discovery, I sent an owner of a business to one of these accountants for some tax advice on a transaction. This particular small business had no accountant onsite; they had been using a bookkeeping service and the bookkeeping service wasn't capable of providing the tax advice required.

When the owner came back to me he said, "The accountant told me I should get seven times profit."

He could have knocked me off my feet with a feather.

I called the accountant and went over to see him.

"Exactly where did you get seven times profit in this case when you've been telling everybody else three and a half times?"

The accountant looked at me with a silly grin.

"Well, you know, we have to allow people to negotiate."

From that point I not only was wary of this particular accountant but any accountant who set a value on a business, either for the buyer or for the seller.

A more recent experience confirmed me in my view that accountants should be kept on defence, leaving the scoring to … me.

24 Keep Them on Defence

We were called in by three partners to value a business. The business had revenue of about $6.5 million and was showing good profits. It manufactured a proprietary product line and only to order. It was a unique business. We set up a value range of between $2.3 million and $2.4 million for the shares of the company.

All three partners immediately said, "Great, let's sell it."

We went to market. We wound up in a bidding war with five different buyers. The final selling price was $3 million.

It was then that we learned why these partners had come to us. It was to verify a value that their accountant had put on their business of $1.2 million.

The three partners had not been getting along. They did not have a shareholder agreement. They were in the process of putting one into place when their lawyers said, "Look, you need to have a valuation done on the business."

All three of them rejected their accountant's valuation. They thought it might be too low because they were thinking the value might be between $1.8 million and $2 million.

A lot of business owners, who after all are usually independent types, feel confident they can handle anything when it comes to their business, including selling it. But often they are simply too close to their business to have an objective view of its worth. That's why it's so important for them to go to outside experts to set a value range for their business.

Sometimes accountants can cost their clients a lot of money, as the next tale illustrates.

25 DAY OF ACCOUNTING

A number of years ago a chap came to us with a distribution business that was operating in three cities. George was seventy-two years old. He ran the main operation. His son operated the second location and an employee the third. We quoted George a fee to do a Comprehensive Business Analysis. He went away to think about it.

George said, when we followed up with him, "No, you guys are too expensive. I'm going to use my accountant instead."

Four and a half years later, just after George turned seventy-seven, his accountant called us.

"Can I buy some of your time?" he asked. "I need your expertise to sort out a problem with George's company."

So Lloyd came in to meet with us. He had three offers on the business: two from competitors and one from George's son. We looked at the offers. We considered the son's offer to be the most significant. We dealt with it first.

I asked Lloyd what the value of the business was. He said that he hadn't done a valuation, which raised a red flag for me, because I thought that's why he'd been hired. I then asked about details on each of the proposed purchasers. Lloyd knew very little about any of them.

"Well, how did you go about getting the purchasers?" I asked.

"I simply wrote a letter to all of the competitors and this is what came in."

I asked our research team to do some quick research on the two other competitive purchasers while I analysed the structure of the son's proposal. One of the things that bothered me about this proposal was that the son didn't have any money. Furthermore, he had arranged financing through a friend of this accountant.

As I probed the financial arrangements, they seemed gray and sketchy and not at all reassuring. Then the researchers came in with the details of the purchasing companies. Lloyd was surprised to learn that the facts about the two companies had been easily discovered in about twenty minutes.

One was very competent and highly qualified to buy. The other one really shouldn't have been considered as a purchaser.

I then insisted on meeting with George. A couple of days later I had dinner with him at a local hotel. George was visibly annoyed with his accountant and blurted out that he had spent $60,000 over the last four years working with him to try to sell the business. Now the accountant had brought me in to bring the transaction to a conclusion. He couldn't understand why it had cost so much to get to where we were. (The costs were now more than four times what we had quoted him on our Comprehensive Business Analysis.)

My next step was to interview the son and figure out whether he knew what he was getting into and whether he was capable. George had doubts about his son's business acumen.

When we interviewed the son we found out he had trouble walking and chewing gum at the same time. While a nice guy and fifty years of age, he really wasn't competent to run a business this size.

We then contacted both buyers and arranged an interview with the one we thought was more qualified. It turned out he had been trying to buy the business for eighteen months but had constantly run into bottlenecks with the accountant.

Within a week we had a new offer on the table, structured so the seller would pay the minimum amount of tax.

The transaction went on to close.

> Accountants may have motives that keep them from providing the best service for their clients. As the next couple of tales show, these motives sometimes stem from protecting their own interests and those of their accounting firm as opposed to protecting the best interests of their clients.

26 AN ESOP's FABLE

We had a very interesting assignment a number of years ago involving a company with operations in four large American cities, all within a three-hundred-mile radius of one another. In three of the cities the company was quite profitable; in the fourth city it was losing money.

We valued the business as a whole at about $4 million for the shares. After considerable research and analysis, we advised the client to close the money-losing operation. We pointed out that by closing that operation they would free up $1 million of capital equipment, which could be sold off, raising the value of the overall business to $5 million.

We were surprised that the company's accounting firm hadn't made this recommendation. We were also surprised that the average accounting fees on a per year basis ranged from $40,000 to $45,000. When we inquired about the accounting firm, we found it was very small, consisting of two accountants and a couple of bookkeepers.

We were subsequently retained to take this company to market. We brought in an offer for $6 million but found that we were running into all kinds of reasons from the client as to why the business shouldn't be sold, all of which seemed to trace back one way or another to the accounting firm.

We arranged to meet with the accountants and the client one day. After a two-hour meeting, we came to realize that the accountants did not want the business to change hands. They wanted to arrange a management buyout by a few key employees, using an ESOP (Employee Stock Ownership Plan).

There are several positive and several negative aspects to ESOPs. They are very complicated. There are people who specialize just in ESOPs because of the legal ramifications of these complexities.

We brought in an ESOP expert to coach us on the value of doing an ESOP. We were told that doing one didn't make sense in this case, because the client was going to take back a note for approximately 40% of the purchase price and provide a guarantee to the employees' bank for the money they were borrowing to pay for the company. However, the accountants convinced the owner to sell the business to three employees.

The owner had to hope that the employees would continue to operate the business successfully.

It all made sense to us when we learned that our client represented about 15% of the accounting firm's total revenue. That's why they didn't want to lose that account. They certainly would have if the business had been sold to a third party.

27 VESTED INTERESTS

We carried out an assignment recently for a lady named Jean who had created a unique business. The business had a number of outlets that were "informally franchised." The valuation of this business took a little more thought than normal because of the potential of selling the franchises. In effect, the business was really a franchising business, not the service business it appeared to be.

We valued Jean's business at about $1.2 million. After making our presentation and giving her the Comprehensive Business Analysis report, we received a memo from her asking us to explain why the accountant didn't agree. Attached to Jean's memo was a four-page dissertation by the accountant explaining to her why our valuation was way out in left field. He stated that the business wasn't worth more than $500,000 or $600,000.

We put a senior analyst on it to review the work of the original team. He came back to us agreeing with the original value we had put on the business.

We met with Jean and explained why our valuation was solid and we weren't prepared to change it, regardless of what the accountant thought.

About three months later we learned the accountant was trying to buy the business for himself.

The best type of accountant to have is what I call a forward-thinking businessperson's accountant. This kind of accountant doesn't just prepare financial statements to tell you how well or how poorly you did in the past.

He or she takes the time to make sure the client is looking forward in their business, based on their past.

Forward-thinking accountants generally prepare a ratio analysis; rolling average sales graphs; and a comparison of your results to those of your peers. These accountants will help you with budgeting and forecasting. They will ask some pretty tough questions to make sure you've thought about some of the things you ought to think about in operating your business.

28 "IF YOU'RE SO SMART, WHY AREN'T YOU RICH?"

In my early years I was quite fortunate to have such an accountant. Whenever I said something he disagreed with, he would look me in the eye and tell me in no uncertain terms what he thought and why he thought it.

His favourite saying was, "If you're so smart, why aren't you rich?"

Whenever I heard that expression, I knew I had done something dumb.

In my first couple of years in the business, he was my mentor, giving me the knowledge and skill I needed to be successful from an accounting perspective in my sales of businesses.

Often when we had a tough question to figure out, he said, "Bring your stuff to the house about at about eight tonight ... and don't forget the case of beer."

I could always go to him and say, "Gee, I've got a problem," or, "I've got this issue. What do you think?"

Because he didn't fear that I would fire him and change accountants, he always told me what he thought. In fact, I think he sometimes wished I *would* change accountants.

In my early years, his tutoring was a big part of my ability to establish a strong financial base for my company to operate from. We worked together for almost thirty years until he retired.

Needless to say, I referred a lot of clients to him and his accounting firm during those years.

Chapter *8*

Lawyers

Selecting a lawyer to represent your best interests in the sale of your business can be a daunting experience in and of itself.

There are many different specialties in law. The law has grown to be so complex that it's not easy to select any one lawyer who has the skills and experience needed for a mergers and acquisitions assignment. Many times an owner requires input from more than one legal specialist.

Think for a moment of the many legal specialties: criminal law (with subspecialties in large and small cases), litigation, litigation appeals, family law, real estate (commercial and residential), contract law, international law, tax law (local, provincial, state, federal, and international), labour law, securities law, environmental law, and a host of specialties dealing with franchise law, corporate law, leasing law, and employment law.

And then there are the generalists who do a bit of everything. Most small-town lawyers are generalists. They can be dangerous to your business health because *they don't know what they don't know.*

When selling the most valuable asset you probably own, don't you think you should get the best help possible?

I know the small-town lawyer charges half as much per hour as the big city specialist (because he has lower overheads), but my experience is that the generalist will take much longer to accomplish the same thing; at the end of the day you may pay the generalist as much or even more than the expert. In addition, you run the risk of having sub-standard legal representation, failing to get one or more of the following (and these are just the tip of the iceberg):

- proper security for unpaid or deferred purchase price
- seller warranties and representations that are reasonable for the situation and will not come back to haunt you after the transaction is closed
- proper terms in leases
- employment / consulting contracts

You wouldn't go to a dentist with a hearing problem. You owe it to yourself and your family to hire competent experts in the field of law appropriate to and needed in selling your business.

29 FLIPPING A COIN

We were closing a transaction in a small rural community in which one lumberyard was purchasing another lumberyard. When it came down to the clause about providing notices to either the purchaser or the seller, the purchaser, Lenny, made a request.

"Could we please insert two locations – my present business, plus the one that I just purchased?"

"No. Take one or the other," the seller's lawyer said.

The two lawyers got into a debate that lasted for about half an hour.

Finally I couldn't take it any longer.

"Gentlemen, here's a Toonie ($2 Cdn)," I said.

I stood up and threw the coin on the table.

"That ought to cover the cost of the second stamp, the second envelope, and the few minutes it takes to make the photocopy and address the envelope. Let's quit screwing around. You just spent $500 of your client's money. Let's just get this deal closed."

The transaction closed and everybody left. I left the Toonie on the table.

I presume the cleaning lady bought herself a cup of coffee.

A great deal of emotion is involved when you sell your business. That makes sense because you have worked in it for a large part of your life. The professionals involved should be careful how they treat the transaction.

30 NEGLIGENCE

We were helping Hans and his wife sell a pool manufacturing company to a group of investors. The investors had their lawyers prepare a formal Agreement of Purchase and Sale. This document was approximately sixty pages long. In my opinion it was well written.

I then met with my clients, who had started the business about twenty-five years earlier and were looking to retire. We went to visit their lawyer, taking the document with us for his review.

The lawyer looked at the document and weighed it in his hand. Then he turned it over, to see who had written it.

"We are wasting your money," he said to his clients. "I have dealt with this law firm before and there is no way this deal will ever close."

He went on to say, "This contract is written so tightly that you will have to get written permission to take a shit."

Then he threw the document on the table.

My clients were horrified. They really wanted to sell their business. They were in their sixties and we had obtained a wonderful offer in terms of value.

I picked up the discarded document and started to flip through it. Everyone sat quietly and watched me read it. I am a fast reader. In about five minutes, I had gone through the whole document.

"I can't find the clause that you just referred to," I told the lawyer.

"What clause?" he asked.

"The one about having to get written permission to go to the bathroom."

"That was just a figure of speech."

"What you said was totally inappropriate, uncalled for, and wrong. Now you get your buns in gear and you do this job right or we'll get another lawyer."

The lawyer pulled himself together. Very few changes were required and the transaction closed soon after.

This lawyer's high-handedness was not a new trait. I learned later that he had mixed feelings about the purchaser's law firm. A few years earlier he been retained by that firm as a sub-agent and had failed to register a mortgage on a piece of property on their behalf. The law firm held him to it and his insurance company had to make good on the mortgage.

> The following tale highlights what can happen when a generalist strays into a specialty where they're not qualified to practice.

31 A TALE OF TWO LAWYERS

We sold Hathaway Couriers, owned by our client, Henry, to Adaptacron Couriers, a competitor that was a hundred and fifty miles away. The two companies, while they didn't compete directly, provided the same services. Their respective markets abutted each other.

Adaptacron, owned by George, was more technically advanced than Hathaway. Adaptacron had computers and a GPS in each of their vehicles while Hathaway operated on a manual basis. Adaptacron was larger and had half as many employees in the office. George, the owner of Adaptacron, saw a major opportunity to use this technology to make the target company more profitable.

We quickly struck an accord and drew up a proposal. Both parties signed. A deposit of $100,000 was placed into our trust account.

George of Adaptacron was to go to his lawyer and have a formal Agreement of Purchase and Sale drawn up. It was to be delivered to us and to Hathaway's lawyer for review.

About ten days later, I received a telephone call from Henry at Hathaway.

"You know, this deal is never going to close," he said. "Please give Adaptacron their deposit back."

"Henry, what are you talking about? I haven't seen the formal agreement."

"The agreement was sent to our lawyer. He said it was a piece of crap and was wasting everybody's time."

I asked him to send me the agreement anyway. It was couriered to me that afternoon.

When I sat down and went through it I was horrified. It appeared that George's lawyer had gone to the law library and retrieved an electronic file of a standard Agreement of Purchase and Sale. This sort of agreement is used mainly for a public, not a private, company.

It looked as if the lawyer had simply started to fill in the blanks. Some of the blanks weren't completely filled in. (I remember there were four different areas where the document said, "Choose one of the four following paragraphs" in italic print – with all four paragraphs still showing.)

I called Henry back.

"Are you still in agreement with the terms and conditions that were outlined in the draft proposal?" I asked.

"Yes!"

"Then let's you, your wife, your lawyer, and I meet and get this matter straightened out."

We met the following day.

In the interim I did some research on Henry's lawyer and discovered that he, too, was not qualified to work on this sort of deal. His specialty was matrimonial law. He didn't have a clue about what an Agreement of Purchase and Sale should look like.

We sat down and started to go through the agreement.

I had marked up the agreement and had attached at least 150 stickie notes to it. After about ten minutes of walking everyone through the agreement, I said to Henry, "You know what? It would be so much better if you had your lawyer write up a proper agreement. He is going to spend more time modifying this than it would take to write a proper one."

I knew full well that his lawyer wasn't capable of doing this. Out of the corner of my eye, I noticed he was gradually turning white.

"I couldn't possibly get at this for three or four weeks," he said. "I'm really busy."

At which time I piped up with a suggestion.

"Look," I said, "we'll have our law firm draw up the formal agreement and coordinate the closing with both you and the purchaser's lawyer."

Then I met with George's lawyer who readily admitted that he specialized in residential real estate and didn't know a lot about buying the shares of a company. I suggested that our lawyer would be willing to guide him through this transaction. It closed four weeks later.

> While lawyers can cause obstacles to a transaction by not paying enough attention to the details, they can also do so by paying *too much* attention to the details.

32 *Undue Diligence*

We sold a small business recently to a large international conglomerate for a selling price of $5 million. Revenues of Donald's company were only $5 million. The company employed approximately twenty-five people. It enjoyed profits of approximately $600,000 a year. The Letter of Intent required a precondition that due diligence would be completed to the satisfaction of the purchaser prior to closing. This is a fairly standard procedure.

The purchaser then asked us if we would assist them during due diligence. Of course we agreed.

Their first request was for us to arrange hotel rooms for ten consecutive nights for six people.

"Why so many people and for so long?" I asked.

I was politely told that this was a standard procedure in the conglomerate's due diligence process.

I suggested that we could help facilitate the collection of some of the information and asked them to send us their due diligence checklist. They faxed it to us an hour later. It was forty-two pages long, single-spaced. There were more than 950 items that they wanted to review before they would close the transaction. Fortunately we had completed a Comprehensive Business Analysis with our client. Most of the material requested was readily available or not applicable.

The whole process lasted one and a half days.

At the beginning of this book I mentioned that the names in some of the tales had been changed not only to maintain confidentiality but in some cases also to avoid personal embarrassment.

Although the next tale caused *me* some personal embarrassment, it has a happy ending. It illustrates the humanness and complexity of people, but in a unique way. In my wildest dreams I could never have imagined this happening to me … or to anyone else.

Every time I think about it, I just shake my head.

33 WHEN THE LOBSTER HIT THE FAN

One of my first transactions was the sale of a chain of fishing supply retail outlets in Northern Ontario. The seller, Dan, was located in Moncton, New Brunswick. He called me up and asked if I would sell these retail outlets for him.

Of course I would. It was my first major transaction since being on my own and I was quite excited about it.

Dan asked me to send him our Listing Agreement. We sent him our standard exclusive agreement, which meant any inquiries from any source whatsoever would be referred to our firm and we would be paid, even if the seller found the buyer. He also asked me for a requisition for all the materials we wanted.

He called me back a couple of days later.

"Doug, this is an exclusive agreement," he said. "I've been negotiating with somebody and quite frankly if he buys the outlets, I don't want to pay you."

"Why don't you finish negotiating with him," I said. "If you can sell them to him – great. And if you can't, then I'd be happy to take on the assignment."

Dan agreed.

I figured I would hear back from him in a couple of days or a week or so. As it turned out, it took longer than that. I waited. No call from Dan. I waited some more and still no call. Six weeks passed.

When I came into the office after a breakfast meeting one Tuesday morning I was told that Dan had just called. I quickly called him back.

"Well, we had a board meeting last night," Dan said, "and we haven't been able to sell the outlets to this fellow. We've decided to give you an exclusive listing, but I'm looking at all the material here, Robbins, and it's a suitcase full. Why don't you fly down and pick it up and we'll sign the Listing Agreement then?"

I headed to Toronto the next morning and hopped a plane for the ninety-minute flight to Moncton. I got there about ten-thirty and I spent most of the day with Dan, collecting all the information. He got me back to the airport at five-thirty p.m. for a five-forty-five flight.

The flight was overbooked and my seat had been given away because I was late.

The nice lady behind the counter said, "Well, Mr. Robbins, you can stay in our beautiful city of Moncton and fly out at six o'clock in the morning or you can leave at eight-thirty tonight, fly through Montreal, and be in Toronto at one o'clock."

I didn't want to stay in Moncton, so I said, "Fine, I'll fly out tonight."

They rescheduled me and Dan took me out for dinner to a lobster shack: one room with four tables and sixteen chairs, a great big pot in the middle, and a Coke machine in the corner. There was one thing on the menu: all-you-can-eat lobster, accompanied by bread and Coke.

"Gee, Dan, too bad my wife's not here," I said as I tucked into my meal. "She just loves lobster. We just got married."

"Well, we can fix that," Dan said.

He went over to the kitchen and asked them to cook and pack up two more lobsters. They wrapped them in paper and put them in a plastic bag and I put them in my overnight shoulder bag.

Soon after that I was in the air on the way to Montreal. Once there I had to take the underground from one terminal to the other to catch my flight to Toronto.

As I got to the second terminal, it was just bedlam. Thousands of people were milling around. It turned out that this was the very first day of airport security in Canada. So they were busy with all the procedures.

I had about fifteen minutes to get on my flight. I could see my plane through the glass wall – a RapidAir flight to Toronto from Montreal. I can be aggressive when I need to be. I pushed my way to the front of the line.

"Excuse me, excuse me, I've got to catch my flight," I said.

The girl at the counter opened up my suitcase with all the documents in it. Then she opened my shoulder bag, took the lobsters out of the plastic bag, unwrapped them, and started to scream. She threw the lobsters up in the air. They hit the ceiling and smashed into pieces all over the floor.

The Mounties were on duty that day and thirty seconds later I was on the floor with a boot on my back and a gun against the side of my head as they secured the airport.

The girl just kept on screaming. Finally they brought out a gurney, strapped her to it, and took her away.

Then the Mounties helped me up from the floor. I had a three-piece suit on. I was covered in floor dust. I was dirty. I was dishevelled. The cleaning crew started to sweep up the pieces of lobster.

And my plane pulled away from the terminal.

"Robbins, you really know how to make an entrance," I heard someone say. I turned around to see someone I knew from a community in Northern Ontario.

"Wayne," I said, "buy me a drink."

"Okay," he said.

Over our drinks I asked him what he was doing in Montreal.

"Oh, my wife and I just came down to do some shopping," he said.

He had come down for the day in his own airplane.

What are *you* doing here?" he asked.

"I was down in Moncton, "I said. "I just listed some fishing supply retail outlets in Northern Ontario."

"Damn. I've been trying to buy those outlets. I couldn't finance them."

"If I could finance them for you would you buy them?"

"In a minute."

"Do you have any room in your plane to take me home with you?"

"It depends on how much Cathy has bought. She's not back yet."

So we had a few more drinks. His wife showed up with some small packages. Very expensive, but very small. So I hopped the flight with them.

By four the next afternoon I had found financing for Wayne to close the deal.

When it comes to closing a deal, there can be disagreements to the terms and conditions. They have to be ironed out before both parties are in accord. Often lawyers are one of the biggest obstacles.

34 AN UNREAL COMPETITION

Agreements of Purchase and Sale often include a Non-Compete Agreement, by which the seller agrees not to compete with the purchaser under certain conditions.

My client, Ron, was selling a chain of four fast food restaurants a hundred miles north of Toronto. Herb was eager to buy them.

We met in the offices of Ron's lawyer. He had prepared a pretty standard Non-Compete Agreement in which Ron would agree not to compete within a five-mile radius of each of the restaurants.

"No, I want a different Non-Compete Agreement," Herb's lawyer said. "I want it to be for the entire province of Ontario."

"I'm happy to give you that," Ron said. "But what about our restaurant in Toronto?" (Ron owned a high-end steak house in the city.)

"Well, you'll have to close it or sell it," Herb's lawyer said.

This was more than a little bit silly. How does a steak house compete with a hamburger joint in the first place, much less when they're a hundred miles apart?

As we moved through the transaction, things got pretty testy between the two lawyers.

Finally Ron's lawyer said, "This is ridiculous."

"You think I'm being ridiculous?" Herb's lawyer responded. "I'm not being ridiculous."

With that he reached over and picked up the bank draft for $1 million and said, "This deal will never close unless you give us a Non-Compete Agreement for all of Ontario."

"This seems a bit silly," I said to Herb.

Herb's lawyer looked at me and said, "Silly? Are you calling me silly?"

"I don't understand how a restaurant in Toronto can compete with a restaurant a hundred miles away," I said.

"Well, this is my advice to my client," he said.

"Doug," Herb said, "I'm paying this guy a lot of money. I don't understand it, but if that's what I gotta do, then that's what I gotta do."

We sequestered the parties in two separate boardrooms. I called my law firm and told them about my problem. They put four researchers in the library and came up with five examples of unreasonable Non-Compete Agreements being struck down by the courts.

I went back to Ron and his lawyer.

"Look," I said, "it's okay for you to sign this 'all of Ontario agreement' and keep your steak house in Toronto because the agreement absolutely ridiculous, unreasonable, and won't stand up in court."

Ron's lawyer headed to his firm's reference library and about forty-five minutes later he and Ron agreed that Ron could sign the document because it wouldn't hold water.

"Sign the one with the five-mile radius, too," I said and they did so.

I took both documents to the second boardroom where Herb was holed up with his lawyer.

"I understand the only issue outstanding, preventing this transaction from closing, is the Non-Compete Agreement," I said. "Is that right?"

"Yes, that's right," Herb's lawyer said in an arrogant manner.

"If we sign that, then the deal is closed?" I said.

"Right."

"Then here is your Non-Compete Agreement for the Province of Ontario," I said. "I now declare the deal closed. May I have the bank draft, please?"

The lawyer looked at the signatures and the document and handed me the bank draft.

I repeated, "I now declare this transaction closed."

"What's he going to do with the restaurant?" Herb asked me.

"Oh," I said, "he's going to continue to run it from Toronto. There's no need to close that restaurant because this agreement doesn't mean anything. It's not valid."

I went on to explain about the precedents my law firm's research team had found.

Herb's lawyer went bonkers.

"They can't do that!" he spluttered.

I looked him in the eye and said, "This document's not worth the paper it's written on. Here are copies of five case laws that render this document totally unreasonable and consequently invalid. Here is the written opinion of two law firms to Ron – this law firm whose offices we are in, plus the law firm I use. We are not here to cause your client any problem."

The irony of the whole thing is – years later Herb's lawyer went on to become a cabinet minister in the provincial government.

> One of the frustrations of dealing with lawyers is getting caught up in myriad discussions concerning where to put the comma. The exceptions are refreshing.

35 NO NEED TO PROVE ANYTHING

We sold a business to the subsidiary of a larger international conglomerate. My clients, Gary and Hugh, were from a small town of 3,500 people. Once the Letter of Intent was signed, I was concerned about the lawyer that they were going to use. The conglomerate was using their in-house corporate lawyer and they had a lawyer from one of the largest law firms in Canada as well.

When the first draft of the formal agreement came in, it was about a hundred and twenty-five pages long. I flipped through it and realized I had a major problem. I felt that my client's lawyer, Hal, was going to be out of his league on this one.

Although I knew that Hal had articled for one of the major firms, I didn't know that he had worked for that same firm for fifteen years in their Mergers and Acquisitions department. Hal was a highly skilled lawyer.

I forwarded the document to him. He read it and called me back.

"I've got half a dozen questions, but it's really pretty straightforward," he said. "Why don't we do a conference call with the other side's lawyers?"

The following afternoon we – Hal, the seller's lawyer, and I – got the lawyer from the major law firm on the phone. In less than half an hour we moved through the issues that had to be dealt with. Nobody was arguing over wordsmithing.

It was a real pleasure to deal with lawyers who knew what they were doing.

It's important to realize when you're hiring a lawyer, an accountant, or any professional consultant that while these people charge fairly high hourly rates, they are really part-time employees.

And the key word here is "employee." They work for you. They are there to give you advice and the benefit of their expertise. They are there also to work in your best interests.

If you had a life-threatening disease, you would want a second medical opinion on the treatment prescribed.

Don't be afraid to get a second opinion if you're not comfortable with anything a professional is saying.

Chapter **9**

I Have No Choice

At the beginning of this book I mentioned that owners can be proactive and take charge of selling their business by constructing an exit for themselves. Or they can delay. Or sell the business for the wrong reasons. Sometimes they have to be helped out of the trench because no other choices are available.

Having to sell a business can involve several factors. Age and illness are just a couple. There comes a time when the owner feels he is ready to pass the baton to the next generation, but delays doing so because he is not quite sure how to do it.

This chapter's tales illustrate the complexity and vulnerability of the human condition when it comes to selling a business.

36 EXTENUATING CIRCUMSTANCES

One day a gentleman arrived at our offices unannounced and asked to see me. I arranged to sit down with him in the boardroom and was amazed at the man's physique. Geoff was approximately six feet four, weighed about two hundred and forty pounds, and did not have an ounce of fat on him. He could have passed for Mr. America any day of the week.

A soft-spoken, deep thinker, Geoff carried himself with great self-confidence.

"Mr. Robbins, I need to sell my business within the next ninety days and I would appreciate anything you could do to help me," he said.

I asked him about the business and could see it was well established and quite profitable.

"What's the big hurry?" I asked him, expecting to hear that he was divorcing his wife or wanted to move on to a partnership situation.

What he said shocked me.

"I have been diagnosed with a rare form of cancer of the white blood cells and my doctors have given me ninety to a hundred and twenty days to live."

I asked whether he had managed to keep this relatively secret and he indicated not really. He had told his employees and expected most of his major suppliers and large customers would know.

I told him that this was a problem. Any serious buyer would be tempted to wait until he had died and then deal with his spouse in order to get a better price. But Geoff asked me to take on his assignment and to do the best I could.

Five months later I delivered an offer to him. I saw him on a Tuesday evening that night to sign the offer. He weighed a hundred and fifty-six pounds.

Geoff passed away the next day.

The bright side of the story is that Geoff did have the foresight to carry sufficient life insurance on himself. His wife and children were financially secure.

Entrepreneurs often struggle with the question, "When's a good time for me to sell?"

Here's a tale about health with an unusual twist.

37 DEATH CONCENTRATES THE MIND

Brad was about to turn seventy and wanted to get Robbinex involved in the transfer of his business to his sons. He was in a bit of a hurry.

It came to light that his father had been diagnosed with Alzheimer's shortly he had turned seventy. Brad had watched his father deteriorate quickly and die shortly thereafter.

Brad was in perfect health but was concerned that he might follow in his father's footsteps. He also knew the chaos that the family had been thrown into when the father had died because his father' affairs were not in order. He felt he had good reason to be in a hurry.

So the Robbinex team got involved. We helped him establish a transition program; empower key employees; delegate responsibilities; and manage the team.

Brad recently turned seventy-five. He remains in perfect health and is still operating his business and thoroughly enjoying himself (and still making a lot of money).

Chapter *10*

The Coke Bottle

Owners can't really see their business objectively.

Let's think of your business as being housed in a giant Coke bottle, which in days of olde was a sculpted green glass bottle. Remember how light coming into these bottles was distorted? First it had a tinge of green and second, everything was out of focus. All you could see were shadows and blurs.

In your business, inside the Coke bottle, everything looks fine. Everything is normal and life is wonderful.

Information comes in through phones, newspapers, faxes, and e-mails. You have a sense of what's going on.

But you're running your business inside your Coke bottle. You don't really see your business in relationship to other businesses, other industries, other countries, other worlds. You see it only through your own paradigm. When the day is over you emerge from your Coke bottle. If you're like most business owners, you're in no condition after a twelve-hour day to do much more than go home. As a result, you seldom get to see the big picture.

At Robbinex we look at a couple of hundred companies every year. So we're not involved in just one or two transactions. We're into a lot of businesses on a regular basis. And we learn.

38 I DIDN'T HAVE TO HEAR A PIN DROP

I've had my own Coke bottle broken a few times, let me tell you. My lawyer takes a shot every once in a while. My accountant does, too. So does my vocational psychologist. He stuck my office in the basement of my building and said it was for my own good. And that's where my office is to this day.

You see, his test results showed my external distractibility measure on a scale of 1 to 100 to be 72, with 16 being normal. This means I hear a pin crash on the carpet a hundred yards away ... and have to get up to investigate.

So I was having trouble getting work done between eight-thirty and five. When everybody was away, I got a lot of work done.

"Your office is in the wrong part of the building," the good doctor said. "You're right next to the phones. You're right next to the secretaries – and to the bookkeepers – and to the front door – and to the telephones – and to the faxes. Everything happens and you can hear it."

The only part of the building that wasn't finished was the basement. We built a soundproof room and they stuck me inside ... where I'm much more productive, I must admit.

While your business may best be thought of as inside the Coke bottle, we your consultants are standing on a very tall ladder in the corner of a beverage warehouse. We can see your Coke bottle. It's sitting in a case of twenty-four Coke bottles on a skid of fifty cases in the midst of many skids of various kinds of beverages. This skid is just one of many that are stacked throughout the warehouse.

Any good consulting business will see your Coke bottle from a different paradigm. We can bring a great deal of objectivity to the business precisely because we are outside it. We are fortunate. Often we have seen your problem before and have provided a solution for it.

39 EMBRACING CHANGE

Many will remember the stock crash in October 1987. It is one occasion I will never forget.

I was standing at a podium addressing about forty-five people in Dallas, Texas.

Someone stopped me mid-flight and said, "Excuse me, Mr. Robbins, but I need to make an important announcement."

He went on to say that the stock market had just dropped 20% and was still dropping.

In less than a minute I was the only one left in the room.

Here's a graph that captures that moment for any investor in the market.

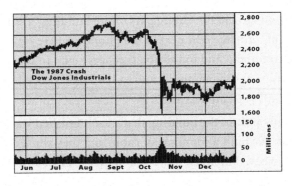

However, the Coke bottle analogy applies here, too. When we get outside it we can see a much different, larger picture of the stock market.

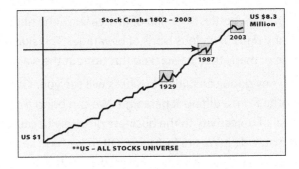

Our world has been changing at a frantic rate. If we were to add up all the knowledge mankind acquired from the beginning of time to 1969, we would have a massive amount (remember it was 1969 when we put a man on the moon). Between 1969 and 1989 all that knowledge doubled. Between 1989 and 1999 it was reported to have doubled again. And it is expected to have doubled again in another ten years.

That is eight times more knowledge than forty years ago.

Just think of some of the things you have today that you didn't have twenty years ago: cell phones, powerful and cheap computers, the Internet. Did you know that your own automobile has more computing power than the spaceship *Apollo*?

If you haven't embraced change in your business, then you may be in for some surprises. You need to surround yourself with competent people and listen intently to what they have to say. There is simply too much happening for you to know it all.

Staying inside the Coke bottle, oblivious to the changes going on around you, can cause a big problem.

40 SMARTNESS IS AS SMARTNESS DOES
A scientist came to me a number of years ago and asked me to sell his company, Scientific Solutions.

Gord was sixty-nine and the go-to guy if you had a problem with manufacturing process or some other issue that science could help you with. He ran a fascinating business with a bunch of PhDs, scientists, and engineers – all sorts of very smart and knowledgeable people.

But Gord needed a solution for his own business. He was eager to tour me through the business and showed me all the facilities and equipment. He introduced me to some of his key employees. He gave me financial information. It was clear that the business was kind of tired. It was old. It wasn't lean and mean and sharp and bright and clean and aggressive. The business was situated on two acres of pristine real estate with a 30,000-square-foot single-floor building. I noticed a large number of empty offices.

After about two hours we went back to his office.

"What do you think you can get for my business?" Gord asked me.

"Well, based on the current level of profitability, it's worth $400,000 to $600,000."

Gord turned beet red.

"Goddam you!" he yelled and reached for some documents on his desk. "I turned down an offer for $5 million five years ago."

He threw the offer at me. The papers went flying all over the room.

Gord put his elbows on the desk, cradled his head in his hands, and started to sob.

I didn't know what to say so I started to pick up all the papers. There were probably eighty to ninety of them. It was an agreement. On the front page, ABC Company offered to buy this man's business for $5 million.

I wondered what I had done wrong. Then I flipped through the papers and at the back found the financial statements for the *preceding* five years. So that almost ten years ago. I had twenty minutes to sit there and read, because that's how long it took Gord to regain his composure.

I engaged him in some small talk. I learned that the number of employees had dropped from fifty-two to twenty-six and that three of his key employees had left to start their own business to compete with him.

I also learned that the principal reason he didn't accept the offer was that he was hoping against hope that his son would take over the business. His son was quite content teaching primary school. Even if Gord's son had the desire to take over his father's business, which he didn't, he was not even qualified to do so.

Gord's business *was* worth $5 million back when he first received the offer, but he had allowed the business to disintegrate – and didn't see that it was disintegrating.

A year later he closed the business, laid off the remaining employees, and sold the building.

> When you are inside your Coke bottle, you may not be able to evaluate accurately the difference between a good offer and a poor one.
>
> Here's a tale of a business entrepreneur who ran his business from inside his bottle … until it came time to sell.

41 DETERMINING REAL VALUE

Winston attended one of our workshops. My sales manager, David, followed up on the phone with him.

"You know," Winston told him, "that was one of the best workshops I have ever attended about selling a business. The workshop was so good that I don't need your services. I just got an offer on my business and I'm going to take it. So thank you very much."

"Well that's great," David said. "How well did you do?"

"I got an offer for book value. That's pretty good, isn't it?"

"I don't know. What's the book value?"

Winston told him it was $1.1 million. Further probing revealed that the company had receivables of $700,000, inventory of $250,000, equipment of $50,000 (at book value), accounts payable of $400,000, and surplus cash of $600,000. The cash was to be included in the sale along with an EBITDA (Earnings Before Interest, Taxes, Depreciation and Amortization) of $450,000 per year.

Winston went on to fill David in on his plans.

"I'm going to get $600,000 in cash, a note for $500,000 payable over five years, and a management consulting contract paying me $125,000 a year for five years. That's a pretty good deal, isn't it?"

"I don't know," David said. "Let me see what Doug thinks."

David arranged to have Winston come in to see us for about half an hour the next day for a quick look at the offer.

Winston brought the offer in, and the financial statements, too.

I looked everything over and said, "You think this is a good offer, don't you?"

Winston agreed.

I called my secretary and asked her to bring me the chequebook. I wrote $1.1 million on the cheque.

"Who do I make the cheque payable to?" I asked.

Winston just looked at me. "What do you mean?"

"I'll give you $1.1 million cash for your business."

"What's wrong with the offer?" he asked.

"You said it was great," I replied. "I'm happy to pay you $1.1 million – no note, and you need to run it for me."

"What is it really worth?" he asked.

"Well, a little more than $1.1 million, but let's sit down and figure it out for you."

It turned out that Winston did need some professional advice regarding the sale of his business. The effect of the transaction he wanted to agree to was that he would be receiving approximately one and a quarter times earnings for his business. Because of redundant cash rules, he would not have qualified for the small business capital gains exemption.

We sold his business to another buyer about four months

later for $2.2 million and Winston got to keep the $600,000 in cash in the company. His employment contract was signed at $150,000 per year for five years.

Of course the first buyer was somewhat annoyed that we got involved, but c'est la vie.

Chapter **11**

It's a Family Affair

If you are like a lot of business owners, you look forward to the day when your son or daughter will follow in your footsteps. It is critical that a detailed strategic plan be developed for their transition into the family business.

Experience has shown us that most business entrepreneurs do not put this task high on the list of priorities when it comes time to prepare a comprehensive exit strategy. In fact, most business owners don't allow sufficient time to complete a proper transition plan at all.

Why does this happen? The answer is: The problem is in the details, or rather the lack of them. Most owners don't prepare a strategy that has sufficient clarity and detail to benefit everyone concerned.

Business owners look at succession planning as a simple and natural progression. However, when the business is kept in the family, this transition is often a very complex process, fraught with unanticipated problems. It is estimated that when a family business is handed down to the next generation (in what's called an intergenerational transfer), the process fails to meet expectations of the participants nearly 80% of the time. A staggering statistic.

There are a number of reasons for this.

Owners forget how much they know and have learned over the years. They are usually unconsciously competent. (See the discussion of the Four Levels of Competence, in chapter 27.) As a result, they are ineffective in teaching, training, and downloading their knowledge to their children. They often underestimate the lack of experience and knowledge of the next generation. They assume that because it's their son or their daughter, they will just know what they need to know.

Their children are supposed to be smart.

They have the family genes.

42 PSYCHED OUT

We received a call from Marella one day. She had just received one of our mail-out pieces inviting her to a workshop.

"I don't want to go to no workshop," she said. "What I want to do is this – I want to transfer my business to my daughters. Can you help me do that?"

I arranged to meet her early the following week. I toured her very nice facility. The business was operating out of 50,000 square feet and was enjoying revenues of approximately $10 million.

Mom and Dad had emigrated from Italy in 1969 and came to Canada with less than $200. They started the business in the basement and within thirty years they had built a remarkable business.

I met their daughters. Anna was twenty-four and single. Angelica was twenty-seven, married, and expecting. It was evident that neither one of them knew much about business.

A psychologist was brought in to interview and test them. The psychologist acknowledged that Anna and Angelica were wonderful women. They would do anything for Mom and Dad, including jump off a cliff. However, they did not have the business acumen necessary to operate a business. The psychologist concluded that if Mom and Dad turned the business over to them, it would fail.

He didn't have to say that this would cause great stress and hardship to all of the members of this family.

The business was subsequently sold to a company listed on the New York Stock Exchange.

> We have a tendency to make our businesses simple. Business owners have a tendency to assume that everybody else around them, especially their offspring, knows what they know. They have run the business in a very hands-on manner and not properly trained the children to become successors.

> The retiring business owner may find it hard to break away ... and may unintentionally sabotage junior's efforts to take control.

43 AN IDIOT'S TALE

We were called in to look at Osborne Ltd., a very profitable company. The business made about $2 million profit a year after paying everybody handsomely. This included the father and mother, Art and Sophia, their children, and their respective families. Art had already survived a heart attack and decided that at sixty-five it was time for him to sell the business.

Our first inclination was to inquire about turning the business over to his son, Jake, who was in his thirties and a vice-president in the company.

"Too f...ing stupid," was Art's response. Sophia agreed.

Osborne Ltd. employed about fifty people. Jake was constantly berated by his father in front of the employees. So naturally they all thought he was stupid.

As we got into the assignment, we decided that we really needed to take a closer look at Jake. I arranged to meet him one Tuesday afternoon about two p.m. and to talk to Art and Sophia after that.

It was a cold and blustery January day when I went to meet Jake. The snow was about two feet high. Jake came walking out of his office wearing shorts and open sandals, no socks, and a Hawaiian shirt. He hadn't shaved in about four days.

"You're Jake?" I stuttered.

We went into his office and I said, "You know what? Your dad has been telling me that you're f...ing stupid, but, you know what? I don't believe him."

"Well, thank you," he said. "Somebody finally believes in me."

"You're not stupid," I said. "You're a f...ing idiot!"

He just stared at me.

"Do you know the difference between stupidity and idiocy?" I asked him.

"No."

"Stupidity is when you don't know any better. Idiocy is when you know better but you do it anyway. What's the matter with you? Why are you dressed like this? Why are you acting like such an idiot?"

"Well, I have to live up to my dad's image of me," he replied.

Talk about a self-fulfilling prophecy.

Jake and I spent nearly four hours together. What an intelligent and insightful person. I concluded at the end of that meeting that he was more than capable of operating the family business.

My meeting with Art and Sophia lasted until about nine p.m. I didn't pull any punches with either of them. I accused Art of treating Jake like a mushroom – keeping him in the dark, feeding him a lot of compost, and then not understanding why he wasn't doing anything.

"Do you know what? That's exactly right," Sophia said and began methodically taking a strip off the old man.

Today, after a two-year transition program, that business is now in Jake's hands. And it is just as profitable as when his parents operated it.

The secret to a successful intergenerational transfer is to create a structured plan as a guide prior to the changeover. The plan needs to be specific to the business and to the family's circumstances. Once potential trouble spots are identified, proper succession and transition plans can be put into place to overcome them.

The goal of a strategic succession plan is to ensure both the well being of your loved ones and the security of your retirement. To make the transition successful, you must develop a comprehensive business plan and complete it well in advance of the day you have targeted to begin life after business.

Sometimes it's hard to let go.

44 PLAYING HARDBALL

During the mid-nineties I got a call from a chap named Grant. He had just received an advertising piece from us promoting one of our workshops. He said he wasn't interested in selling; he wanted to buy his father's business.

Grant was forty and had a degree in civil engineering and an MBA in marketing. He had joined his father in the family business in the early eighties when the revenues were only $3 million and there was barely enough money for each of them to live on.

In the mid-eighties Grant went back to school and got his MBA because he realized that the business needed professional management. Since that time the revenues had increased to $43 million, a direct result of his efforts.

Owen had become passive over the past five years. There had been an understanding between father and son that Grant would take over the business for a proper consideration. No one knew what "proper consideration" meant.

They had spent a lot of time and about $150,000 in professional fees trying to set up a structure. But in the end, Owen just said no.

Grant told us he had just given his father his resignation and would be moving two hundred miles away to start his own business. He went on to say that his mother was devastated because the move would mean she would seldom see him and his three young children. Owen was perplexed. He couldn't understand why Grant was leaving a job that was now paying him $250,000 per year. Owen was also being paid that amount.

We met with Grant and Owen a week later and were warmly received. We conducted a series of meetings: one with both of them; one with Grant; one with Owen; and a fourth meeting with both of them again. It was agreed that Grant didn't really want to leave the business and Owen didn't want him to. What was needed was an orderly transfer of the business from father to son.

The problem seemed to be Grant's three sisters and how they could participate in the value of the business. One sister was a nurse and two were teachers. Owen had suggested that the business be divided into five equal shares: one share to himself and his wife, one share to Grant, and one share to each of Grant's sisters.

Grant objected. He was doing all the work – why should his sisters share equally in the profits?

We started conducting a comprehensive review of the business, which included interviews with their lawyer and accountant. Both the accountant and the lawyer noted that they had had great difficulty communicating with Owen.

We valued the business at $7.5 million. We recommended an estate freeze whereby that amount would be converted into special shares and placed into a family trust. Documents were drafted to summarize the details of this arrangement. Grant signed. Owen hesitated, saying he wanted to discuss this with his lawyer and accountant. That was fine by me because I knew that the lawyer and accountant had already given their blessing to this plan.

Several weeks went by. Even though Owen wasn't playing an active role in the business, he still claimed he hadn't found the time to visit either his lawyer or accountant. As I pushed him to bring this to a conclusion, I detected the probable reason for the delay.

Owen was seventy-five but looked sixty. He wasn't ready to admit that he was getting old. I arranged to meet with him and his wife, Sheila. It was an amicable meeting and in the end, Owen agreed to proceed. I pulled out the document and asked him to sign. Once again he refused.

It was time to play hardball.

"How are you going to operate the business without Grant?" I asked. "If Grant opens up in competition with you, what effect will that have on your business?"

I turned to Sheila and asked, "How will you feel when Grant and his family move so far away? You won't be seeing your grandchildren very often."

The two of them sat there, speechless.

Sheila finally turned to her husband and simply said, "It's time, Owen. Sign the papers."

Chapter *12*

Trouble Spots

Potential trouble spots come in many shapes and sizes. For example, the business owner may see their offspring through rose-coloured glasses as perfection incarnate. Or they may perceive them as virtually useless.

The problem of perception may extend to the offspring. They may have an inflated view of their capabilities.

This next tale from the trenches has some interesting dynamics.

45 **THERE'S ALWAYS A WAY**
Approximately fifteen years ago, a long-time business associate, Ralph, invited me to lunch. I had done a number of consulting assignments for his firm over the years.

"I would like you to sell my business now," he said. "I am sixty-eight. It's time for me to put my affairs in order."

"What about your son, Jimmy?" I asked. "If I'm not mistaken he's been working for you since high school – about twenty years now."

Ralph became very quiet. Finally he said, "I'd like nothing better than to have my son follow in my footsteps, but he has refused."

"Why?"

"I don't know. It would make me very happy to have him take it over, but Jimmy's made it very clear to me that he wants nothing to do with the ownership of the business."

"Let me at him," I said. "I'll have him straightened out in no time at all."

Jimmy and I had a couple of beers late one afternoon a week later at his golf club.

The bottom line was that Jimmy lacked confidence. He didn't have any money either.

"Look, the value of this business represents my dad and mom's retirement," he said. "I don't want the responsibility of failing and destroying their retirement program. So just sell it."

I felt a little dejected. I had failed to convince him to do what I thought was a sensible and natural thing to do.

We took the business to market and found a buyer. Four months later, we had an acceptable offer from that buyer. So we proceeded. The buyer wanted to have an opportunity to talk to the son – alone – for a couple of hours as part of his due diligence. We were fine with that.

They started their meeting at ten in the morning. The meeting lasted sixteen hours – until two the following morning.

The buyer called us and said, "I'll buy the business only if Jim signs a five-year employment contract. As an incentive for him to sign the contract, I'll give him the first right of refusal to buy the business from me."

"That's strange," I said. "How is that going to work for you?"

"Well, Ralph's sixty-eight. I'm fifty-two. Jim's thirty-eight. I'm right in the middle. I'm trying to arrange it so I don't have to pay you a commission."

I laughed.

"That's good thinking. That's forward thinking. But what's the real reason?"

"Jim is quite capable of running the business. He knows all of the customers, suppliers, and employees. He's managed the inventory and administrative functions of the business. But he doesn't have much knowledge about the financial aspects of the business. I believe in five to seven years I can teach him all he needs to know, at which time he can buy the business from me. And I won't have to pay a broker's fee."

I went back to Ralph and said, "Do you know, this is not a bad offer. But I would like to take one more shot at your son. I would like him to be assessed by a vocational psychologist."

We made the arrangements. The psychologist came back and said that Jimmy was lacking in self-esteem, because he had been kept in the shadow of his father over the years. He hadn't even met the company's bankers. He didn't understood balance sheets or the company's cash-flow processes. Jimmy was petrified to take on this particular responsibility.

As I became aware of the problem, I remembered that Jimmy's younger sister, Isabel, was a certified general accountant. I called and arranged to meet with her.

To make a long story short, I arranged for Jimmy and Isabel to become partners, on a 60-40 split (with Isabel owning 40%). They took over the business from their father. The company's bank financed the transaction, putting close to $1 million into Ralph and his wife's retirement fund, ensuring a financially sound retirement for them.

Ralph broke down in tears, he was so happy.

The previous buyer was kind of ticked off, though ... but that was okay. We found him another business.

> Sometimes the next generation trains for something outside the field of the family business.
>
> Here's a tale with a unique twist.

46 A SALE ... AND A REUNION

We were called in to value a most unusual business. It had revenues of $5 million and pre-tax profits of $1 million. It carried no inventory, no A/R, no furniture or fixtures, and operated out of a rental facility of approximately 2,000 square feet. The company purchased components and assembled them and shipped them to their customers under their own trade name. At the end of the day this company's biggest asset was its trade name.

Phil, the owner, was about fifty-eight. He really wanted to put his feet up and retire.

We initiated a Comprehensive Analysis on the business and came up with a figure of $5 million, which was composed mostly of goodwill. We told Phil that in our opinion, we couldn't sell the business without seriously compromising it.

He looked at me strangely.

"Well," I explained, "as soon as we tell a prospective purchaser about your business, that purchaser can simply go out and source the product from similar suppliers; run advertisements similar to yours in similar magazines; take the orders; package them; and ship them. Why would a purchaser want to pay anything for something that they can easily replicate?"

We recommended that he run the business for another couple of years and then quietly close it down.

This left Phil in a bit of a quandary.

I understood from our initial discussion that Phil had a daughter who was a corporate lawyer living in another province. I suggested that she might take over the business.

"I don't think so," Phil said. "I haven't talked to Patty in five years."

I inquired why that was the case and he quickly explained,

"I divorced her mother. When her mother moved to another province, Patty went with her. I haven't spoken to her since she left."

Further probing revealed that in Phil's eyes, Patty was extraordinarily competent and undoubtedly could run the business.

"Give me a budget of $5,000 and let me see what I can do."

I got Patty on the phone a couple of days later.

"Do you have your computer on?" I asked her.

She did, so I had her go to the Robbinex website.

"This is who you are talking to," I said. "I am in a position to offer you an opportunity – provided that you are competent, capable, and passionate – that will make you $1 million profit a year for the rest of your life. At this point I cannot tell you who your benefactor is until I am confident that you are both willing and capable of running a business."

I told her I had arranged for a first-class return ticket for her to Toronto on Wednesday. I invited her to call Air Canada to verify that this was true. I gave her the confirmation number and told her I had arranged for a limousine to pick her up and take her to the Sheraton Hotel in Toronto where a suite had been reserved for her.

"On Thursday," I continued, "you will meet with a vocational psychologist. He will have you write a couple of tests and ask you a bunch of questions. And based on his recommendations, a determination will be made whether the offer is made."

"Is this some kind of joke?" Patty asked.

"Call the airline, the limousine service, and the hotel. And call me back within half an hour to confirm that you will be on that flight."

Patty called me back and confirmed that she would be on the

flight. She wanted to know more about the situation. I refused to tell her anything.

"After you meet with the psychologist you will be returned to the airport. You will hear from us within a week or so."

Needless to say, Patty passed the psychological assessment with flying colours. Ninety days later, she was the proud owner of a very profitable business. She not only came back to be with her father, but she brought her husband with her. Phil didn't know that she had married.

About a year later, she delivered Phil's first grandson.

> It's amazing the kind of trouble spots that come
> to light when someone is ready to sell their business.

47 WIN-WIN

It was a mid-sized auto dealership. Ward had suffered a debilitating health setback. He had three sons and a daughter. The daughter, Lucy, was married and very well off. She didn't really care about the business. Two of her brothers, Ryan and Brent, were in the business. Gerald, the third son, was in another profession. He felt slighted that a company car hadn't been provided to him gratis by his father or one of his brothers.

As I got involved I found out that in all those years Dad never owned the business 100%. He had a silent partner. So we had to deal with that partner, too. We also had to take the deal to the major car manufacturer.

The manufacturer said, "We want them to upgrade the building. They need to spend about $2 million on that. And after they upgrade the building, we'll transfer the franchise to one of the sons, not both. You've got to pick which one. And if we don't like the one you pick, we are going to take away their franchise. You've got thirty days to solve the problem. Have a nice day."

And to add a little more excitement, Dad had cancelled his $2 million life insurance policy on the advice of his insurance broker. Absolutely dumb. I don't know whether the broker worked for the insurance company or what, but fortunately we have a law in Canada that if you cancel, you can reinstate it within a certain period of time.

In fact, we got Dad's insurance policy back within a week of the expiration of the reinstatement date.

A vocational psychologist was called in. He interviewed the family – Dad and Mom, sons and daughter, daughters-in-law and son-in law. Then we called in the family's lawyers and accountants.

The psychologist had his work cut out for him because both brothers wanted the dealership. It made a lot of money. The psychologist learned that the younger brother, Brent, really wanted to be in a different business but didn't have enough money to acquire it.

We rented a boardroom at a local Holiday Inn for a family meeting. All ten showed up along with the family accountant and lawyer.

We said, "This is the way we see it. We will reorganize the business into two companies: a holding company and an operating company running the dealership. Ryan will own the voting shares of the operating company and manage that business. The holding company will provide funding/ guarantees for Ryan to acquire the dealership and also provide funding/guarantees for Brent to acquire his own business. Does anybody disagree?"

The silence was golden.

Chapter *13*

Family Feuds

The next generation doesn't always have the temperament for leading a business. If more than one child is in a leadership position, situations may develop in which sisters and/or brothers battle among themselves for control or power to make decisions.

Sibling rivalry can be particularly problematic if ownership or control is not given to the most capable.

48 Two Visions, Two Wins

I was speaking at a Rotary club one evening and was approached by an accountant at the end of the meeting. He told me about a huge dispute being waged between two brothers over a food distribution business with revenues of over $40 million.

The father, who had recently passed on at the age of eighty-eight, had given equal shares about ten years earlier to each of his two sons, Harold, forty-nine, and Stanley, fifty-two.

The brothers seemed to get along while the father was alive. Before his passing, Father would come into the business most days for a few hours.

It turns out that Harold's son, Eddie, and Stanley's son, Jason, both wanted to become president. The turmoil between the cousins embroiled their respective fathers in the family feud after their father had passed on. Two sets of lawyers,

accountants, and valuators had been retained. An accor
seemed impossible to reach, even after $300,000 had bee
spent in professional fees.

I agreed to meet Harold and Stanley separately to see il we
could be of assistance. I reviewed the valuations (which were
apart by about 20%). I spoke with both sets of lawyers and both
sets of accountants. I then called in our vocational psychologist
to meet both brothers with a view to determining which one
should buy and which one should sell.

Stanley really had a passion for the business and had
developed an extensive seven-year plan for taking this company
to the next level. Harold had no such vision and had no time for
the older brother's plans. It turned out that Harold just looked
on the business as his personal ATM.

Further discussions with the psychologist revealed that
Harold saw himself as a consultative expert on privately held
companies. He really wanted to sit on the boards of six to eight
smaller companies to which he could pass on this wisdom.

When we illustrated how he could use the money received
from selling out to his brother to buy into a number of smaller
businesses and provide them with the benefit of his knowledge,
he was eager to move into a new stage in his business career.

Once the findings were in, it became fairly straightforward
to bring both brothers to a satisfactory agreement.

Family feuds come in all shapes and sizes. Here's an
interesting tale about one family feuding with another.

49 LOST IN TRANSLATION
Many years ago I was the chairman of a BIA
(Business Improvement Association) in my community. There
were one hundred and eighty-two businesses in this association,
run by owners who seemed to come from every country in the
world. One day the Portuguese owner of a business on the street

approached me asking if I would mediate a dispute between him and his Italian neighbour.

Apparently they had been arguing over an issue for many months and had decided to find someone to help solve the problem. I asked what the problem was and he said I should hear it from both sides at the same time. A time was set to meet at Joe's Banquet Centre down the street.

I arrived at the appointed time to find an eight-foot table placed strategically in the centre of the very large banquet hall, with four chairs on each side and one chair at the head of the table, presumably for me. I sat down and a few minutes later the Portuguese businessman arrived with his wife, son, and daughter. A couple of minutes later the Italian fellow arrived with his wife and two sons.

I shook everyone's hand and asked the Portuguese chap to tell me what the problem was. The Italian immediately interjected, saying that he would tell me, from his point of view. In a loud voice, and in Italian, he proceeded to tell me what was bothering him. Before I could interrupt to explain that I didn't speak Italian or Portuguese and ask if we could all speak in English, the Portuguese chap started to respond to the Italian ... in Portuguese.

Before I knew it, the hall was filled with the echoes of everyone speaking loudly in their respective languages.

All of a sudden the Italian family got up and caucused in a corner of the hall. A few minutes later they returned to the table.

The father spoke to the Portuguese businessman in Italian. And then everyone nodded and shook each other's hands and thanked me profusely for mediating. They left the hall, everyone happy.

To this day I don't know what the dispute was about.

"What do you want to be when you grow up?" is one of my favourite questions for business owners. They usually give at me a strange look and laugh.

"Yeah, you've got a good point," they say. "I guess it's time for me to decide that."

We all grow up in different ways.

50 A MAGIC WAND

A banker was put in a difficult position with two partners who were fighting. The only thing he could do was call in their loans, because their business was making no money.

"I don't know if you can do anything about this," he told me, "but I recommended that they talk to you."

"Am I to call them or are they going to call me?"

"I told them to call you. So let's give it a couple of days and see if they do."

One of them, Terry, did, so I said, "You know, Terry, I can't help you unless your partner agrees."

After Scott, his partner, called, I sat down and had a long chat – one-on-one – with each of them.

It became clear to me that they were not compatible.

Terry and Scott had married sisters. These brothers-in-law were as different as black is from white. And the sisters didn't share philosophies either, whether it was about life or about business.

Needless to say, the brothers-in-law didn't get along. They started this little business. They wound up with three stores. The stores were just making a half million bucks profit a year before they started fighting.

So I said to Terry, "What would you do if I could wave a magic wand and put half a million bucks in your pocket?"

"Oh, man," he replied, "I want to be a musician. You know, I'm a good singer and I play the guitar and I'd build a studio in my basement and ..."

I asked Scott, "Hey, what would you do with that money?"

"I would start another business and compete with my brother-in-law."

So it was obvious who was going to buy whom. Scott borrowed enough money from the bank to buy out Terry. Terry took the money and built a recording studio.

Terry never did make it big time in the music business. He wasn't a great singer, but that's part of life. Now he's out working for somebody else, but he's happy. He received enough money to pay off his house and set himself up for life. He doesn't have to work too hard. And he did have his fling with his band.

The key to this interaction was nothing more brilliant than getting these men to ask the "when you're grown up" question.

Chapter *14*

Partner, I Hate You

The life expectancy of a partnership is about three and a half years. They don't last very long. Partnerships are born because the people involved have come together for a purpose and a goal. At the beginning of the partnership, everyone is excited and enthusiastic about the purpose and the goal.

When things don't work out the way they envisioned, they become stressed and disappointed. Problems occur; arguments become part of daily life; and disillusionments finally make the partnership die.

When the business is struggling, the partners are struggling, too. But when it starts to grow, oftentimes one of the partners is working much harder than the other one and feels he should be entitled to more of the profits.

Over the years we have become involved with some of the most amazing partnership issues – some of them have been absolutely mind-boggling.

51 DOOMED TO FAIL

A number of years ago, I was called in to a small food-processing business run by two partners, Greg and Tim. Greg phoned and explained that they were having major partnership problems. He was wondering if we could do something about it.

I said I thought we could and asked him some questions about the business. Then I interviewed Tim, who begrudgingly and warily told me his side of the story.

I found that there were irreconcilable differences between the partners regarding how the business should be run. It was a high-profile business in the community, one that commanded great respect. It was expanding rapidly.

In valuing the business, I discovered that, if they were willing to keep the business for a couple of years longer, its value would more than double. Consequently, I went back to both partners with a suggestion.

"If there's any way at all to resolve your problems, or at the very least, declare a truce, you can both benefit greatly. There's a surge in demand for your product, but you're going to have to get along for a while."

After more than fifteen meetings, one-on-one and together, we reached an accord on how the business could be operated over the next twenty-four to thirty months, at which time it would be taken to the market and sold.

I clearly remember the final meeting . It was on a Monday evening in Greg's home. We didn't finish until almost ten. At that time we reached an accord and we all shook hands. Tim left. I was gathering up my documents and preparing to leave when Greg's wife arrived.

She asked what had happened and Greg explained the truce, along with how they were planning to manage the business for a short time before selling.

Flames shot from her eyes.

"There's no f…in' way that that's gonna happen. I want that guy and his b…h of a wife out of my business immediately."

The whole thing blew up right then and there.

While there appeared to be two partners, in reality there

were four. And the two women not only didn't like each other, they couldn't tolerate being in the same room together. It turned out the fundamental problem was between the two women, not the men. Each told her man what to do and how to do it.

As a result, that business was sold about four months later for an amount far below what it was actually worth. Instead of getting $1 million each, Greg and Tim got $300,000 each.

The partnership was doomed to failure before it began because neither Greg nor Tim had given any thought to the behind-the-scenes roles that their wives played.

> The cost of setting up the correct structure for operating and ultimately terminating a relationship is low compared with the financial and emotional cost of unravelling a relationship that no longer meets the original needs of the partners.

> Terminating a business partnership is rather like a divorce. When there's no prenuptial agreement, the situation can become very messy and costly indeed.

52 CUTTING LOSSES

I remember one company we were asked to help. The two owners were fighting, but they were very proud of the business. I toured the business with Walt, one of the partners. It was quite a nice little business that did about $3 million of revenue a year.

Walt took me in to meet his partner, Steve.

Steve turned out to be rather cold. He wasn't really pleased that we were talking about selling the business.

"Well you guys have to agree, or I'm not working for either one of you," I said.

"Yeah, I guess," Steve said reluctantly. "The shareholders' agreement says we have to do this, so I guess we have to."

"Can I read the agreement?" I asked. "That's a very important document."

Steve pulled out a big, thick document. It was about forty pages long.

I sat there and read it. When I got to the last page I said, "I presume that you guys have a copy that has been signed by both of you."

"Let me see that," Steve said. "That's the only copy I've got."

Walt got up and went to his office and grabbed his copy. It wasn't signed, either.

"I've got you, you son-of-a-bitch!" Walt said to Steve.

And the business was dismantled, just like that – totally dismantled. They hated each other that much.

An extreme example, but it happens.

> A partnership dispute can create raw emotions – emotions that can easily lead to a total lack of common sense.

53 STUCK HERE IN THE MIDDLE ...

I had to have the police called in once when I was dealing with partners. I was the only thing between them and their fists.

The partners, Jack and Bob, owned a banquet facility. Things generally are quite slow in such businesses during the week and weekends hectic. Big parties can leave big messes to clean up.

It seems that Bob was seldom available for the clean-up detail on Mondays and Tuesdays. Washrooms can also be messy and the day I first met with them, a Wednesday, Jack was yelling at Bob that it was time he did some clean-up work and he could start with the washrooms.

Bob wanted to know why Jack hadn't cleaned them by now – after all he had all day Monday and Tuesday. Jack shoved Bob and Bob shoved back. It was time for me to leave. On my way out I had one of the employees call the police.

Jack and Bob had been partners nearly four years and, needless to say, the ending was not too happy. The bank called the loan and appointed a receiver.

What you see is not always what you get.
Appearances can be deceiving, as this next tale illustrates.

54 LAST WORDS

I was once retained to sell a rather small business, with revenues of less than $1 million. It was run by two partners. They had two other employees. The partners had been together for nearly thirty years. Lonnie, fifty-six, was in charge of production and manufacturing. Clive, sixty-nine, was in charge of sales and marketing.

The company manufactured a very niche product line. Its manufacturing equipment was somewhat out of date. This made the overall sale difficult. In fact, it took almost two years for us to find a buyer and close the transaction.

I was always amazed at the congeniality of the partnership. The two fellows individually spoke highly of each other. They seemed to work well as a team. The business never earned a lot of money, but both partners earned a decent living of approximately $100,000 a year.

After introducing the business to approximately twenty-five different buyers, I finally found one who was prepared to move ahead and make the acquisition. He had delivered a very good offer.

I was surprised to experience difficulty in getting a response from the two partners. After two and a half weeks, the buyer was ready to withdraw his offer and look for another business, due entirely to the partners' lack of response.

I finally had to force a meeting between the two partners.

I had to become quite aggressive, at least in terms of getting a response. I wanted to find out why they weren't responding. After all, we had already walked numerous buyers through this business and hadn't gotten very far.

It turns out that Lonnie didn't really want to sell. Clive was having some health issues and needed to put his affairs in order. Finally, we did reach an accord and a transaction was struck, with the deal closing approximately three weeks later.

The closing itself proved to be unusual as well. It's one that I'll never forget.

We met in the office of one partner's lawyer. This office was located in a majestic old home. After the closing we walked out the front door and down the eight steps to the sidewalk. I was standing on the porch with Clive. Lonnie, the buyer, and the buyer's lawyer had already reached the sidewalk.

"Excuse me," Clive yelled without warning. "There's something I've been meaning to tell you, Lonnie."

Everyone stared as Clive launched into a venomous tirade about how nasty and miserable Lonnie had been and how much the older man had hated working with him for the last thirty years. The language he used is not fit to print.

Clive accused Lonnie of purposefully ruining the value of the business by slowing down production and by turning down jobs, preventing the company from reaching its full potential.

This, reasoned Clive, had effectively denied him the type of retirement he would have had if the business had been worth more money.

I hoped Clive felt better after he got that off his chest. As for me, I felt better knowing my job was over.

Not every partnership is doomed to failure. Some can endure. Here's a tale with a different kind of ending.

55 PARTNERING BY THE RULES

I was once called in to put a partnership together.
Two chaps, each with a retail store and each with a small service
centre attached to it, wanted to join forces.

Zack and Arthur had been friendly competitors for many
years, with their businesses being located at opposite ends
of the city. They had decided that if they became partners
they could buy better. They could also spell each other off for
vacations. In general they thought the businesses would do
better together than apart.

I'm not a strong proponent of partnerships, since many
partnerships fail within three or so years and very few are still
going after seven years. So it was with some reluctance that
I sat down and structured the partnership.

It was to be a newly incorporated company. The new
company would buy each of the businesses from the two
partners. Arthur's business was larger than Zack's. It had more
inventory, higher sales, and higher profits. So we valued Zack's
business at $250,000 and Arthur's at $350,000. We issued shares
in the new company. Each partner ended up with 250,000
common shares. Arthur ended up with 100,000 special shares.

The arrangement on the special shares was that they were
to receive a dividend and they were to be redeemed prior to any
other disposition or action on the common shares.

We then sat down and carefully crafted the responsibilities
of each partner and their respective stores, hiring new
employees, and so on. After that we negotiated remuneration,
because both their wives also worked in the businesses.
We negotiated reasonable vacations and when they would be
taken and how the business would be run when one of the
partners was on holidays.

The negotiation process and the structuring process took

approximately six weeks. We ensured that all the bases were covered and no issue left untouched.

We took the recommendations to a lawyer, who drew up the contract; incorporated the company; issued the respective shares; did the shareholder buy-sell agreement; created the company by-laws and detailed the authority and responsibility of each person.

That was in 1985.

That business continued to thrive for twenty more years, at which point the partners came to us again, having decided that it was now time to sell. We were pleased to sell that business and help both partners retire.

They told us that during their partnership they virtually never had an argument; that the rules, regulations, procedures, and responsibilities that we had crafted had worked well throughout those twenty years. They each got their vacation every summer.

Their businesses thrived and one business was relocated to a better part of the city, causing an overall increase in sales.

In the end, the business sold for enough money for both partners to retire comfortably.

> The moral of the story: If you're going to enter into a partnership, it is imperative that you take the time to do it right. I highly recommend the use of a vocational psychologist, who can assess the personality profile of each partner to see if they are indeed compatible.

56 WHEN IT'S BETTER NOT TO WED

I once represented a client with a small machine shop that took in revenues of about $1.8 million. The owner introduced me to Joe, a salesman who sold cutting tools to my client. He told me Joe was interested in buying the business.

Joe and I got together. One of the first questions I asked was, "How much money do you have?" followed by, "How are you going to operate the business?"

Joe said he and his neighbour, Tony, were going to "partner up" to buy the business. Tony was going to operate the shop and Joe was going to be in charge of sales.

They did not strike me as compatible. I encouraged them to meet with our psychologist. His professional opinion supported my gut feeling.

And, fortunately, he convinced them not to become partners.

Chapter *15*

Failing to Plan?

Failing to plan can end up being planning to fail.

In this book I emphasize how important it is for clients to think the whole process through with an intermediary. I like to think of people following what I call a 10/5/3 planning program.

First is the **ten**-year vision – looking ahead to where you personally want to be in ten years' time. In order for you to be where you want to be at the end of that period, you then have to ask yourself, "Where does my company have to be in ten years?"

Once you establish that ten-year vision for the business, you need to say, "All right. What do I need to accomplish in the next **five** years? What goals do I need to reach within the next five years if I am to have any hope of reaching the ten-year vision?"

After you establish what those five-year goals are, you sit down and do a detailed business plan for **three** years – quarter by quarter – regarding what you're going to do with your business to achieve the five-year goals. That way you will have a chance of reaching your ten-year vision.

The next thing you do is a one-year detailed business plan, month-by-month and line-by-line. You lay out what you're going to do. The next step is to measure your activity by what happens monthly against what's planned for the year. And you make the appropriate adjustments.

You also need to have a business valuator evaluate your business. The valuation doesn't have to be complicated, as long as it's done consistently, using the same methodology each year.

So once you've got the 10/5/3 program in place, every year you need to do it again. Because at age fifty you're going to be looking at yourself doing things at age sixty that are not the same things that you are going to be thinking about doing at age seventy. And during those ten-year spans, the world will be changing.

When you're first putting a 10/5/3 planning program together, allow a sufficient amount of time so you can cover all aspects of the process. An important part of this process is to be detail oriented and to be forward-looking. You must remember that this is a *learning process* as well as a planning process. You will be learning about your business and its potential and opportunities. Consequently, the first-year business plan needs to be reviewed monthly – actual results against plan. It is quite likely that at three months or six months you will need to revise the plan to reflect the reality of what is actually happening.

The real value of the 10/5/3 planning program will be realized only when you make annual updates. As you move into years three, four, and five, you will recognize that the ten-year year vision is actually changing, albeit very gradually. Your accuracy in planning will also improve and you'll be surprised at how accurate your forecasting will become.

During all of this there will be changes in technology, competition, markets, products, and employees, to mention only a few. *The only constant today is change,* and these changes need to be identified and worked into each segment of your 10/5/3 program.

Sharing your program with members of your advisory board will bring forth dozens of questions, thoughts, ideas, and alternatives for you to consider. This process is precisely what's behind the strategic plans of highly innovative and successful businesses.

I had lunch recently with a client whose sales six years ago were $800,000 and had hovered in that range for almost ten years. Today, after implementing a 10/5/3 strategic plan with the help of his advisory board, his sales have increased to almost $4 million.

You've got to recognize that as time moves on, so do your goals and aspirations, and so does the economy, and business, and technology, and people ...

Sometimes you don't see this change because you're operating day to day inside your Coke bottle.

57 CRYING OVER SPILLED OIL

An owner, Jackson, approached us to sell his small machine shop. It was absolutely pristine, located in a brand new 10,000-square-foot building, situated in a farmer's green ten-acre field. It also featured a paved driveway and parking lot and was well landscaped.

We recommended that a phase one Environmental Impact Study be done prior to going to market. The client inquired what the cost would be. I said it wouldn't be a great deal, probably $2,000 to $3,000. Hopefully we'll get a clean bill of health, I told him.

To my surprise, Jackson was perturbed by this.

"You know, I built this building myself," he told me.

"This has always been farm land. There's never been anything polluted on it. I'm not going to spend that money. Just go and sell my company."

We found a buyer, who put in an offer, but the offer required an Environmental Impact Study for the buyer to obtain financing. When the impact study came back, it demanded intrusion testing, which involves drilling boreholes in order to take soil samples.

I approached the environmental engineer and questioned the need for the drilling. He took me to the back of the machine shop and showed me a stain on the wall where it met the floor. It was approximately twelve feet wide and extended up the wall by about six inches.

The engineer explained that the machine operator at a screw machine in that part of the shop had hurt his back some time ago and had felt it wasn't necessary for him to carry his waste cutting oil up to the front of the building where the central disposal was. He had been meticulously and carefully pouring it down the crack between the wall and the floor.

The drilling revealed that the cutting oil had seeped approximately eighty feet into the ground. The oil had hit an underground spring, which carried it off the property.

We had to initiate a clean-up. This involved drilling holes into the ground around the machine shop. Water was then back-pumped into the holes. It was then vacuumed back up through filters and finally recycled through the ground. This process took roughly ninety days before the ground was relatively clean.

During that period of time, a firm in Cincinnati acquired Jackson's major customer. This customer accounted for 40% of Jackson's sales. As a result, the customer's plant was moved from Ontario to Cincinnati and Jackson lost the business. His sales dropped by 40%. His profits went from a comfortable level to zero. The value of the business dropped significantly. In addition, the clean-up cost him almost $300,000.

Had the Environmental Impact Study been done six months earlier, we probably would have caught that problem before it became serious, prior to going to market. Also, the business would have been sold prior to the loss of the major customer.

And Jackson would have retired with much greater financial resources.

To leave work after thirty-five or forty years may sound like a great idea. You may be ready to go. But when you begin to consider the reality of what life will be like after retirement, the uncertainty can be pretty intimidating. If you haven't planned, you may be dragging your heels. You may have to be hauled out of the trench.

We often hear how important it is to prepare a business plan. A good business plan is like a road map. It's about the future. It shows you where you are and where you are going. In preparing a business plan, unexpected issues may surface. They have to be addressed.

Here's a tale about an element of planning that an owner didn't foresee.

58 STALEMATE

I looked at a business a number of years ago that was quite profitable. It manufactured, remanufactured, and repackaged products. The products were sold to the hardware industry. Victor was enjoying sales of about $5 million a year, showing pre-tax earnings of approximately $350,000.

It's interesting to note that Victor had bought an old schoolhouse. He was using the facility as his office and manufacturing facility. He used the gymnasium as his warehouse. He turned the classrooms of this small school into his office, a reception area, and a boardroom.

The flaw in this situation was that the business and the real estate were owned by the same company. A purchaser came along who wished to buy the business but didn't want to buy the real estate. He offered what appeared to be a very attractive lease for ten years.

Victor wanted to sell the shares of his company in order to enjoy the capital gains exemption. To do that he needed to dividend the real estate out of the company. That meant he would have to have the real estate appraised; pay tax on the recaptured appreciation of the depreciated portion of the real estate; and pay capital gains tax on the increase. Then he would have to pay a dividend distribution tax on the amount he dividended out. The real estate was worth about $1 million and the taxes to move it out were about $350,000.

The alternative was to sell the assets of the business and retain the real estate inside the company. However, that meant recaptured depreciation tax on the equipment along with capital gains on the equipment, which would result in a large amount of tax.

As a result of poor tax planning, the business was not sold.

There are some psychological and people factors that need to be considered along with all of the financial and economic and business factors. Business owners are interesting and intriguing people who have struggled with all kinds of issues related to selling their business.

Businesses should have a primary strategy. Many also have a secondary strategy that can add to the net worth of the company.

Some businesses have no strategy at all.

59 TURNAROUND ARTISTRY

I received a call from a lawyer friend of mine a few years ago asking if we could help one of her clients. I went up and met with Matt and his partner, Walter.

I have never seen a business in such bad shape. Poor administration, poor sales, poor leadership, and poor manufacturing and production. Yet in spite of all that, these partners had a really viable product line.

I called my retired banker friend and asked him if he would like another turnaround assignment. He was open to the idea so we went in to take a long hard look at the company.

The company was virtually bankrupt. Although it had good products, it had dug itself into a hole so deep it was unlikely it could ever crawl out.

Our analysis indicated that the 20,000-square-foot facility they had leased was far larger than what they needed. They probably could operate out of about 8,000 square feet. We also concluded that they were running with at least 50% more employees than required given the company's sales levels and the production functions.

The two partners were shareholders and didn't get along with each other. Our psychologist's report indicated they would probably never agree on much. That added a new set of dimensions.

Matt had loaned the company approximately $150,000 and had the foresight to take out a general security agreement.

We called in a trustee in bankruptcy and put the company through a power of sale (a receivership), using Matt's secured loan as the means. We put the business into a new company; moved to a new location of 8,500 square feet; dropped the partner, Walter; negotiated with a new bank; and dropped half of the employees.

Today this company is alive, well, and profitable.

Chapter *16*

Advisory Boards

Operating any business today is far more challenging than it was even just ten years ago. With today's explosive growth in knowledge, new technologies, medicines, and communications, the world as we know it is changing at a fantastic rate. It is unreasonable to expect that any one person can keep current with changes in laws, taxation, rules, and regulations. Then there are changes in equipment, software, production methods, offshore competition, new sources of supply, financing, new products, new ways of manufacturing. The list of changes goes on and on.

One of the most effective and inexpensive ways for businesses to address the huge changes affecting them is to establish a board of advisors. The advisors should be drawn from many different disciplines:

- business
- law
- accounting
- engineering
- sales/marketing, etc.

They can bring much intelligence to a small business, often making the difference between profitability and outright failure.

Many small independent business people join or form groups of people from similar-sized businesses and different business segments (to avoid competition issues) in order to learn better business practices from each other. These groups usually meet six to eight times per year for a full day and often bring in outside speakers on topics of mutual interest to the group. Most progressive franchise companies now offer group programs to their franchisees so they can learn from one another to improve their operations.

60 No Substitute for Good Advice

I have known Bob, the owner of a fruit-processing plant, for about twenty-five years. Bob is the fifth generation of his family in the business. It started out as a fruit farm that grew by acquiring other fruit farms and then gradually began processing the fruit. Over the years the business grew significantly.

I learned that Bob had made an acquisition of a similar operation in the US. I later heard through the grapevine that the integration of the acquisition was going poorly and that the overall business was losing money. I contacted Bob to see if I could be of any help.

When we met he told me he had recently joined a group of business owners. They were now giving him some good advice. Bob and the business owners had created a local executive advisory board of five business owners with similar-sized businesses, a transaction lawyer, and a forward-thinking accountant.

Bob went on to explain that the group had been formed a short while ago. They had had two meetings and were developing a business plan. And as such he didn't think he needed any more help at this time.

We stayed in touch from time to time and it was amazing

to observe the effects the local advisory board on Bob's business. Needless to say, it turned around in short order and the money-losing acquisition was subsequently resold.

Automotive manufacturers and their dealers are very strong on advisory boards. Most dealers belong to a group made up of approximately twelve to fifteen dealers, from the same manufacturer but all from different markets – again to factor out competition.

They share the most intimate of operating details. The groups are designed to assist each dealer to be aware of all aspects of their business as compared with the peer group, of which they are members. All of the financial results are then pooled to create a series of standard operating results. Each dealer can then compare itself with that.

61 THE COURAGE TO ASK FOR HELP

We had an auto dealer client who faithfully attends a dealer group. However, Larry had a problem. Another dealer in his territory who sold the same product had hired away his general manager, who in turn had hired away three additional key employees. They had also taken a computer copy of his customer list and were now contacting his customers, inviting them to the competing dealership.

My immediate reaction was to initiate legal action and apply for an injunction to stop the competitor from using the list to contact his customers. Larry was horrified at the thought of suing another dealer of the same manufacturer. He initially refused to consider that course of action.

As it turned out, a group dealer meeting was coming up within a week. I asked if he had discussed this problem with them.

"No, I haven't. I'm too embarrassed to."

"Embarrassed is no excuse not to protect your business," I exclaimed.

I made him promise to discuss this problem.

Larry called me on his way home from the dealer meeting. He had brought up the problem and the group was not only unanimous in support of him but emphatic that he take legal action immediately. In fact, two of the dealers said they would call him within a couple of days to make sure he had engaged a lawyer. Did I know a good lawyer?

We arranged a meeting with a litigation lawyer within a couple of days. A computer expert was brought in to determine how the customer list was removed and by whom (believe it or not, this can be done). And a lawsuit was initiated against each of the former employees and the competitor.

It was determined that the former service manager was the culprit who took the customer list from the computer.

Within a relatively short period of time, a large cash settlement was agreed on. The customer list was returned. Copies were destroyed. And a covenant not to approach any more of Larry's employees was issued. Within six months all of the employees who had been poached by the competitor were no longer working there.

Three of them had asked for their old jobs back, but none was rehired.

To this day, I don't believe my client would have taken legal action, no matter how much I insisted, without the encouragement of his dealer group.

> It has been my honour and pleasure to sit on numerous boards over the past thirty-five years. I can tell you that a good advisory board will almost always ensure that you're looking at the big picture for the long term.

62

THE VALUE OF GROUP HONESTY

I know a mid-sized business owner wi'
about $50 million who had pulled together a gr'
business owners with similar-sized businesses f.
North America.

All the businesses were in different fields of endeavour,
but at that size, business operations, accounting, taxation, law,
marketing, advertising, employee issues are all similar.

The nine business owners in this group met four times a
year for an average of three days. Each paid his own expenses,
took turns hosting, and never charged the others for their
time. They shared financial information, product information,
marketing information. Nothing was held back.

This business owner said he never left a meeting of the
group without significant new ideas to implement in his own
business.

He added that all the other owners felt the same.

Many franchise companies now have similar peer
group meetings. Organizations have been created to
facilitate the coming together of like-minded business
owners to exchange experiences, challenges, and
successes.

63

SPRINGBOARD TO RICHES

A number of years ago a man named Rick called us to
sell a division of his company. As we began our Comprehensive
Business Analysis, we started hearing that the business was not
operating very well. While sales were in excess of $100 million,
pre-tax profits the previous year were only $100,000. Rick's
EBITDA was only $500,000.

His banker was not comfortable. Employee morale was
relatively low. And we learned that Rick was seldom there.
He had excellent accounting and tax support from his public

ounting firm, an excellent lawyer, a decent banker, and a number of key employees who were all concerned about Rick's lack of "leadership."

Once we had completed the Comprehensive Business Analysis, one of our recommendations was for Rick to form an advisory board with two of his key employees on it. The board met alternate Monday mornings for four hours over a period of eighteen months and then scaled back to one meeting a month. We were pleased to be invited to sit on that board and watched the progress unfold as the business plans were put into place, implemented, and then realized.

The two key employees were properly motivated by an incentive program based on profit-sharing and had the support, guidance, and vision of a powerful advisory board. They supplied the leadership that had been deficient.

And two years later the business earned $5 million of pre-tax profit.

It's important that the professionals who become part of your advisory board are prepared to work as a member of the team and not create their own team.

I have a board of advisors here at Robbinex composed of five men and women I respect.

64 IRON SHARPENS IRON
I went in to my advisory board one morning and said, "I want to do this, this and this."

And they said, "But have you thought about these other things? And what about this? ... And why don't you focus on that?"

They pushed me really hard and made me rethink a number of initiatives I was contemplating.

If the old cliché, "Two heads are better than one," is true, then five heads are even better than two.

Chapter *17*

Don't Cook the Books

Integrity is a huge issue when it comes time to sell a business. Many times in small cash businesses the owner will let you know that the books don't tell the whole story. As they begin to tell you that "X" dollars in cash have gone unreported, they believe that the buyer or intermediary will be impressed with their cunning.

Not so. What the owner has just told you is that they are *a liar, a cheat, and a thief.* Who wants to deal with someone with those credentials?

65 AVOIDING THE TRUTH

A number of years ago, we were called in to talk to the owner of a business, about the possibility of selling his Canadian and American operations. After about a forty-five-minute discussion and a quick review of his financial statements, Norm took us on a tour of his facility.

As I walked through the facility, I saw a warehouse filled with inventory. My quick estimate was that it was worth about $1.5 million. As we walked through the machinery centre, I estimated the equipment there could be worth at least $500,000 to $600,000 any day of the week.

We went back into Norm's office. I opened up his company's balance sheet and said, "You know what? It would appear as though there is an error in your inventory. You are showing only $250,000."

Norm was a pretty self-assured guy. Almost cocky.

"No, there's no mistake. I just don't report it. If I had to report it, I'd have to pay tax. And if I pay tax, I couldn't carry as much inventory as I have. If I couldn't carry as much inventory, I couldn't sell as much as I do. And therefore I wouldn't make any money."

We then looked at the equipment. The book value of the equipment was about $45,000 with an initial cost of about $150,000. Again, I queried this because I thought the equipment was worth a great deal more.

Norm replied, "It certainly is worth a lot more. But I buy the parts for the machines and charge it to my cost of sales. And then I have my guys go in there during slow times and assemble the parts I bought. They have made the equipment that we currently have."

"According to my estimates," I said, "your equipment is worth between $500,000 and $600,000."

Norm agreed.

As we looked at the corporate structure, I noted that he had incorporated an offshore company and was funding sales to that company. All in the name of saving income tax. At the end of the day there was virtually no tax being paid by this corporation.

I looked the chap in the eye and said, "You know, we have a major issue here. We do not have the avoidance of income tax. We have a major income tax evasion. And to be quite candid, I want no part of it. You evaded taxes on $1.25 million worth of inventory, on about $600,000 worth of equipment, and in the labour used to assemble that equipment. Now you're funneling sales through an illegal offshore company. Frankly, I can't think of anyone who'd buy your business with all these contingencies in it. And I respectfully decline the opportunity to sell it."

I suggested to him what he needed to do over the next five

years was to either dispose of that inventory or bring it into the balance sheet of the company. Same thing with the equipment. I sent him to a tax specialist with respect to his offshore company and to tidying up his balance sheet.

I indicated this clean-up would probably take five years before his company would be in a position to be taken to market.

Dishonesty comes in many forms. Here's a tale with an outcome that few could have imagined.

66 STASHING THE CASH

Many years ago, I sold a business that manufactured its goods in a small, neat, clean, and tidy facility. Above it were living accommodations for the owner, Ivan. On weekend jaunts, Ivan would travel throughout the province and set up sales stands in various flea markets and church halls.

He had three rotating routes and did quite nicely on this route business.

Ivan was asking for a fair amount of money for his company. I had great difficulty with the price, based on the revenue and profits of the company. We finally found a buyer. Andy was ready, willing, and able to buy Ivan's business.

When questioned about his revenue and profits, Ivan said, "Oh my gosh! There is no problem proving to you that the profits are much higher than shown. Let's go to my bank."

Andy looked at me and we all jumped into this old rattletrap of a vehicle and drove down to Ivan's bank. We walked into the safety deposit box room. Ivan opened a safety deposit box and showed us almost $100,000 in cash.

He went on to explain that all the revenue that came in from his weekend route business went directly into the safety deposit box. Once a year, he flew back to the old country and took this money to his parents. Ivan was due to make the trip again in about six weeks.

Seeing this extra cash Andy quickly agreed to Ivan's asking price. The transaction was consummated. However, part of the deal was that Ivan stay for ninety days in order to show Andy the ropes and teach him how to operate the business.

During the tenth week after closing of the transaction, Andy and Ivan became embroiled in a very heated discussion. This resulted in some shoving and pushing.

Andy was pretty steamed. He called Revenue Canada's 1-800 number. The following morning the RCMP showed up at Ivan's bank with a warrant and a locksmith. They drilled into the safety deposit box and removed the cash.

Ivan was never heard of again.

Here's a tale whose outcome has an ironic twist to it.

67 *Too Clever by Half*

I was involved in selling a hi-tech machinery company a number of years ago. The owner, Barry, told me the inventory was undervalued by maybe $100,000 to $150,000. I inquired why, expecting him to tell me about some sloppy business practices.

Instead, I heard an intriguing tale.

It seems that during an economic downturn, business was really slow and cash flow was awful. When Barry went to the bank on a Friday afternoon to cash his paycheque, the bank refused to cash it because the company was overdrawn. It had cashed the other employees' cheques. Obviously the banker was trying to get his attention.

Later that evening, he had to borrow some money from his foreman to buy groceries for his family.

From that day forward, Barry always kept (in his words) a "reserve of inventory that could be converted to cash on a moment's notice if the money was needed." With the book value of inventory being about $500,000, I didn't think that the undervaluation would pose much of a problem.

We sold the business about six months later to a large American conglomerate. They worked the weekend prior to the Monday closing counting and valuing the inventory. I was at the lawyer's office on Monday morning when Barry walked in all smiles and exuberant. The inventory had been valued at $1.5 million. He was ecstatic.

Just then the representatives from the buyer walked in with their chins on the ground, announcing that they were unable to complete the transaction because of the inventory problem. (They were purchasing the shares of the company and would therefore inherit any tax liabilities.)

Their comment was, "We are foreigners here and we have no intention of finding out what your jails are like."

The Twist:

Barry had left his wife on Friday evening; bought a new Cadillac on Saturday morning; and his girlfriend was in the car waiting for the deal to close so they could head to California.

The Outcome:

The transaction closed with the inventory valued at $600,000. Barry went off to sunny California with his new car and his girlfriend.

The Irony:

Had the inventory been properly accounted for during the past five years, the growth in inventory would have raised the profits of the company, thereby increasing its value. The balance sheet would have reflected this increase in the value of the inventory.

I calculated that had Barry done things properly, he would have most likely sold the business for $1 million or more.

At the end of the day, the business intermediary is

selling the owner's credibility as much as the business. If the owner is credible, the buyer will feel more comfortable in making the acquisition, and will be less concerned about "surprises."

In effect, as the comfort level increases, so the risk decreases. As the risk decreases, the earnings multiple used to establish a value goes up.

68 THE RISK OF DISHONESTY

This company was in the business of selling and servicing equipment for small to medium-sized companies. Revenue was approximately $2 million with the sales being split equally between equipment sold and service on existing equipment. Everything in the operating company looked normal except the cost of sales, which seemed a bit high.

As we probed into the anomaly of the cost of sales, we discovered that there was a warehouse approximately half a mile away from the main operation. It contained brand new equipment that had been purchased and paid for by the company. But it was not counted in the inventory. The value of the equipment was $500,000.

We pointed it out to Quinton, the owner of the business. We told him this created a bit of a dilemma. "If you disclose this to a prospective purchaser, and then the transaction doesn't go through for any reason, the purchaser would probably call the 1-800 number. He will likely register a claim with Revenue Canada. They would then pay the purchaser a bonus on any taxes they collect from you. At the end of the day, Quinton, you are at great risk."

We urged him to clean up his inventory before he took the business to market.

When integrity is lost, it's almost impossible to get it back. Sellers who "cook the books" have misrepresented their company. They are dishonest. They are no longer trusted. Any potential purchaser will lose confidence in the seller and walk away from the deal, or try to buy it at a very low price.

69 WHEN IT RAINS, IT POURS

Many years ago we were selling a large manufacturing business that was housed in a 150,000-square-foot building. It was situated on ten acres in a small Manitoba community. The business was operating at about 40% of capacity and was barely profitable. It had substantial assets, but selling these for a reasonable value with low profits was going to be a challenge.

One thing that intrigued me was the fact that the owner insisted that we insert into our profile of his business the fact that they had a special roofing program.

There had also been a spill of a toxic chemical that was cleaned up. They had an engineer's report to that effect.

We searched the world for a buyer. We found a Japanese company that saw the opportunity to put additional production through the plant. We reached a tentative agreement subject, of course, to due diligence. For the Japanese firm, due diligence was important – and they were extremely diligent.

They arrived with a team of engineers to go over the equipment in fine detail. On the third day there was a severe thunderstorm. The rain was teaming down. One of the buyer's engineers came into the boardroom soaking wet. His boss said to him, "Don't you have the sense to stay inside when it's raining?"

"I was inside," the engineer protested.

We all went to see where he was when he got wet. Beside one of the machines, a steady stream of water was pouring through the roof.

"What about this roof program you're so proud of?" the vice president asked.

Our client sheepishly said they were a few years behind.

Nonetheless, the Japanese company was still quite interested in proceeding with the transaction. But they no longer trusted the client to be truthful. His integrity was destroyed. They now double-checked and triple-checked everything they were told. They discovered many irregularities. They were still interested in spite of the irregularities. Then they brought in drilling rigs to test the property for toxic chemicals.

Guess what? That toxic spill had been cleaned up only locally around the spill point. Parts of the property were so badly polluted that the purchaser walked away. The deal was never completed.

I believe that had the client been forthright about all of the issues and not tried to hide anything, the sale would have been consummated because the Japanese company really wanted that facility.

> This next tale should be called "covert operations."
> A dishonest business owner discovers the domino
> effect … the hard way.

70 UNDER THE RESTAURANT TABLE

Early in my career I was selling a mid-sized restaurant in a shopping mall. It was a nice restaurant, family style, licensed, table seating of a hundred and twenty with ten bar stools. The statements showed a reasonable profit, not great, but reasonable. Food costs seemed a bit high. So did the labour costs. We found a buyer who was preparing an offer and wanted to see the business one more time before he finalized his offer.

We arrived at the restaurant about nine-thirty on a Tuesday morning to find the restaurant closed and the bailiff's notice on the door.

Further investigation revealed that two tax inspectors had been casing the business for about six weeks. One had breakfast at the restaurant every morning and the other lunch. During that time, they had befriended the owner and watched his activities carefully. They noted the average meal ticket size and the average number of customers daily.

They calculated that the owner had been under-reporting his revenue by about $2,000 per week. That's over $100,000 per year. They assessed him approximately $100,000 for taxes not paid over the past three years and an additional $100,000 in penalties. A total of $200,000.

However, things did not stop there. The owner complained to anyone who would listen. The shopping centre owners got wind of what had happened. They were to be paid percentage rent and they had not been paid their 8% on many hundreds of thousands of dollars. They cancelled the lease and seized the equipment.

I did not complete that sale.

Chapter *18*

When Is Enough ... Enough?

Some people want to die with their boots on. And that's fine. You can have big, heavy-duty work boots. You can have really nice cowboy boots, because you own a dude ranch. Or you can have sandals on the beach. It doesn't necessarily mean you have to be wearing your work boots when you die.

Business owners need to have the opportunity to think about what else there is to do with their lives. Do they want their business to consume their soul for their whole life?

- When is enough ... enough?
- How much money is enough?
- How much stress is enough?
- How many arguments with clients are enough?
- How many employee issues are enough?
- How much fighting with suppliers is enough?
- How much fighting with unions is enough?
- When have you had enough?

71 AN OFFER YOU SHOULDN'T REFUSE
Oscar came to visit us one day. He was jittery and said he had just about had it with his business. He wanted

to sell. Oscar informed us that he was asking $2 million for the company.

He added that he was quite proud of the fact he had just turned down $1.2 million for it. In fact, he was quite indignant that someone would offer him such a low price for his company. He proudly announced that he was quite rude to the purchaser, using language we can't include in this book.

In reviewing his statements, I noted his revenue was only $850,000 per year with an EBITDA of approximately $100,000. There were no fixed assets because it was primarily a service company.

I was concerned that I was missing something significant because the business appeared to have a value of only $250,000.

I called in our senior evaluator and asked him to cast his eye over the financials and tell me what he thought it might be worth. He said $250,000 to $275,000.

Oscar started to shake. Tears welled up in his eyes as he realized he had made a terrible mistake.

Further research revealed that the purchaser was in the process of doing a rollup, with a view to creating a public company. As such he was prepared to pay a premium to acquire certain firms that would have both strategic and synergistic value when combined.

We contacted the purchaser. We apologized for our client on the basis that he was under a lot of tension and didn't know what a good deal he was offered. We convinced the purchaser to re-offer.

We closed that transaction within three weeks.

Burnout is a very real problem and shouldn't be taken lightly. It's a state of emotional and physical exhaustion. It's caused by excessive and prolonged stress. Burnout reduces productivity and saps energy. It leaves its victim feeling hopeless, powerless, and resentful. Burnout can threaten jobs, relationships, and health.

It certainly affects a business owner's judgment.

72 When a Rest Is as Good as a Change

We were approached by a forty-five-year-old chap, David. He had gone into business with his father, Jordan, some fifteen years earlier. Jordan was now seventy-five years old. David said he wanted to sell the business in order to straighten things up with his father. They currently co-owned the company on a 50/50 basis.

As we looked at the company we found that the sales growth was steady at 14% to 18% growth year over year. Current revenues were approximately $15 million. Profits were well in excess of $1 million after paying wages of $250,000 to both Jordan and David. Jordan was not active in the business.

The company had a really unique product line and a niche market. They had the products manufactured for them offshore – with light assembly, packaging, and shipping within four hours of receiving an order. The products were brought in under their trade names and re-marketed. Customers believed that our client actually manufactured the product.

I suspected that David was suffering from burnout and just wanted to get out of the business. I brought in a vocational psychologist to interview and test him.

The psychologist advised that David was extremely burnt out and was close to a mental breakdown.

When it came time to present results of our Comprehensive Business Analysis report I insisted that David bring his wife and his father to the meeting. I wanted Jordan there, because he was 50% owner. David's wife needed to be there because she owned half of whatever David owned. Also at the meeting were our analyst, our valuator, and our psychologist.

We went through the presentation. We showed the three of them what the business was currently worth and how long it would take to sell it. I then turned to David and said, "I'm not prepared to take this business to market until you take a four-week vacation that is totally isolated and uninterrupted – no cell phone, no laptop."

"I can't possibly do that," he said. "I couldn't get away more than a couple of days at a time."

"Do you know what will happen if you get sick or have a heart attack or an accident? Who will run the business then?"

David pondered that for a few minutes and said, "Well, I guess Dad would have to come in and operate the business until I got better."

I looked at Jordan and I said, "Can you? Are you willing to come in and operate the business for the next three or four weeks to give your son an opportunity to recover from burnout?"

"Absolutely," Jordan said. "When do you want me to start?"

I then turned to David's wife and said, "Can you find a place to take him where there are no telephones and no Internet?"

Her eyes sparkled and she said, "Try me."

I then told David that until such time as he had this vacation I was not prepared to consider taking his business to market.

About six weeks later he called me and thanked me profusely for forcing him to take the trip away from the business. He had managed to get away for only two and a half weeks. But during that time he had an opportunity to rest, recover, and recuperate.

"You know, taking that vacation was the best thing I ever did," he said. "I had a chance to rest and clean my head out. Now I know I don't want to sell."

He listed the reasons why he no longer wanted to sell the

business. They were all good business reasons – economic reasons, not emotional, burnt-out, tired, psychological reasons.

Most business owners want to make sure they sell their company for the best possible price. They have worked hard for many years and want to ensure that they will have a comfortable retirement. Yet for some business owners, money is not a factor at all. They have a very different definition of "When is enough enough?"

This is a tale about one of the most fascinating assignments I ever had.

73 THE COST OF RUDENESS
As a result of one of our workshops, a fellow came up to me and asked me to help him buy his company back.

"Well, tell me what that's all about," I said.

"My name is Adam and I own only 20% of it. A firm in France owns the other 80%. When I started my business, I ran into difficulties and they provided some financial assistance. They gave me a pile of money and took 80% of my company. I want to buy it back. They don't want to sell it to me."

This was definitely shaping up to be an interesting case.

"I've learned that the whole company in France is now for sale," he continued. "The owner is seventy-nine years old and I heard that he wants to sell. I've got all of my friends together and I have $44 million. We want to buy that company from him. Would you go over and present the offer?"

I said yes and over I went.

Unfortunately, the owner in France didn't speak English. So I called the Consulate and I said, "Hey, Canadian Consulate, I've got a problem. I need an interpreter and I need a really good one."

I got one and off we went.

I met with Marcel. His son, Jacques, was there. Jacques was forty-nine or fifty years old. We all got involved in a discussion about whether Marcel should sell his company to my client or not.

Now this company was not only in France and Canada, but also in the US, Mexico, China, India, and Italy. Excellent company. In the course of the conversation, it came out that Marcel had received an offer for $30 million from a friend down his street.

So I am sitting there with a $44 million offer and he's sitting with a $30 million offer. The $44 million offer is from an adversary, somebody he bailed out and called "ungracious." The $30 million offer is from a friend of his.

"I need to think about this for a couple of days," he said. "Can you come back on Friday?"

That was Wednesday. So I came back on Friday with the interpreter.

"Mr. Robbins, you have caused me great, great stress during the last two days," he said. "You know, I figure I'm going to live to be eighty-nine or ninety years old. I have calculated how to spend the money I receive when I sell. I've decided I'm going to give my worthless son here a couple of million dollars and I have figured out how I can spend the rest of the money over the next ten years. But you know, I couldn't figure out how to spend the other $14 million, so I'm not going to accept your offer. Thank you very much. Goodbye."

My mouth fell open wide enough to drive a truck through it.

> Money is called a great motivator. Not every business owner believes that.

74 WHEN IT'S NOT ABOUT THE MONEY

I took a phone call from a chap who had received a Letter of Intent from someone who wanted to buy his business.

Drake said he was dealing with a guy who was jerking him around. I told him what he should do about his Letter of Intent.

Tear it up and find another buyer.

Drake was sixty-nine. He had a terminal disease. He might have four or five years left, but the business was suffering as a result of his poor health. Three years earlier his sales were $25 million. Now they were $18 million. We thought his business was worth probably $5 million or $6 million.

Drake then made a quick decision. He called a competitor and sold for $4 million just because he didn't 't need it.

"What am I going to do with an extra $1 million or $2 million?" he asked.

Money no longer was what was motivating him.

Chapter 19

Sixty-Eight Hours? Not Me

Most entrepreneurs work at their businesses an average of sixty-eight hours per week. I refer to it as the Entrepreneur's Week.

Here's a little tale from the trenches that may serve as a mirror and/or a wake-up call for entrepreneurs about the lives they're leading.

I know this trench very well.

75 THE REAL COST OF OWNERSHIP

The first reaction to my description of the Entrepreneur's Week is, "No way, not me. I don't work sixty-eight hours a week."

Let's just think about that for a minute. Monday through Friday, from the time you get up – say at six-thirty a.m. – until you return home – say at six-thirty p.m. – you're thinking about your business.

As you're having breakfast, you're thinking about your day.

On the drive to work, you're thinking about your upcoming issues.

During lunch … well, lunch is often with a customer or supplier.

And, if you are lucky, you leave shortly after your employees, usually about five-forty-five or six p.m.

On the drive home you're thinking about tomorrow. Then, that evening, you may read a business magazine, an article, or a report. ("Just relaxing," you say.) Usually on the weekend you sneak into the office for a "couple of hours" which usually winds up to be four or five hours (don't forget your travel time).

And on the other day of the weekend, you may be at home but you're just doing a "few minutes" of paper work. Or perhaps you are relaxing, playing a round of golf with a business associate, or your lawyer or accountant.

And don't forget those trade shows and conferences. Those activities are often sixteen or more hours per day of just go-go-go: three to five days for each conference, sometimes two or three times a year. You can't really miss those conferences because your competitors will be there talking to your customers. Of course, if you are running a booth, there are the long weeks of work preparing for the show.

Oh, of course you take your cell phone and laptop with you on vacation, just in case you are needed (which you usually are, but only for a moment or a few hours here and there).

Add it up and see how close you come to the sixty-eight number. At some point in your life, you will have had enough of the sixty-eight-hour week.

> Despite the hardships and the stress, some entrepreneurs realize that they are not yet ready to give up their long workweek.

76 BUSINESS IS GREENER ON THE OTHER SIDE
I retired one guy, Darren, at age thirty-seven. Millions of dollars in the bank. He had done very, very well. Within a year of the sale, however, he was pulling his hair out, begging me to sell him a company. Anything at all.

"I've just got to get out of the house," he said. "My wife's going to kill me. I'm going to kill her. I hate it!"

And yet six months before he sold his business he was yelling, "Get me out of this business. This is terrible! I gotta work twelve hours a day. I gotta work six days a week. I don't want to be here anymore."

He went through this scenario over and over again until we finally found a buyer for him. But now Darren had nothing to do and no longer had a sense of purpose in life.

We did find a business for him about six months later.

Suffice it to say that Darren no longer complains about the Entrepreneur's Week.

Chapter 20

Ignorance Is Not Bliss

The true value of a business lies in the future profitability of the business as seen through the eyes of a buyer. This is the principal reason we never post an asking price on any of the businesses we represent.

77 Choices, Choices

We once had a business for sale that we felt was worth about $800,000. After many months of marketing this business, we received four offers within a few days of one another.

Each buyer had taken the time and hired professionals to assist in valuing the business from their point of view. The range in proposals was startling, to say the least.

1 $300,000 cash on closing

2 $600,000 with $300,000 cash on closing and a $300,000 note over five years

3 $900,000 with $800,000 cash on closing and a $100,000 note over one year

4 $1.3 million with $300,000 cash on closing and the balance over ten years if the business continued at its current revenue levels.

Which offer would you accept?

There's an old expression, "Loose lips sink ships."

Sometimes loose lips can sink a good sale, too. Here's
a tale of an owner with loose lips.

78 A SIN OF COMMISSION

I was working on selling a machine shop and the
client, whose name was Trevor, had already gone through the
phase one Business Analysis process. We valued the business at
$1 million, which was approximately $400,000 over book value.
The machinery and the equipment were heavily depreciated.
The cash flow supported a selling price of $1 million.

I located a buyer approximately two months later. The
buyer visited the facility; looked at the equipment; reviewed the
financial information in the profile; and indicated to me that he
thought the business was worth $950,000 to $1 million.

"Great," I told him. "You should put in an offer."

"Yes," he replied, "that's a good idea, but I'd like to go
through it one more time and take my plant manager with me."

I arranged for a tour of the facility for a second time on a
Thursday evening. The buyer arrived not only with the plant
manager, but also with a partner, his accountant, and his
equipment appraiser. Five of them in all. The plant was only
about 15,000 square feet.

As the entourage toured the facility, Trevor became
separated from our Robbinex salesperson and wound up having
a one-on-one conversation for a few minutes with the buyer.
On Friday morning our salesperson called the buyer in order
to solicit his proposal. He wouldn't return his call. We tried
several times on Friday, then again on Saturday, and once
again on Monday, to no avail.

Late Monday afternoon I received a call from a lawyer friend
of mine.

"Hey, Doug," he said, "I see we're doing a deal together."

"Oh, really, what's that?"

"We're buying Trevor's machine shop."

"Oh, great. Have you put together the Letter of Intent?"

"No, we've got the formal agreement done and it's been signed by both sides. We met with the seller and his lawyer on Saturday. It's all done and signed about an hour ago. All I have to do is negotiate your commission."

"I don't know if I understand what's going on."

"Well, my client asked Trevor what he wanted for the business and Trevor said, 'Give me the book value and you pay the broker.' So they cut a deal for $600,000."

Before Trevor's one-on-one conversation during the plant tour, the buyer had been prepared to pay up to $1 million for the machine shop.

Trevor's loose lips lost him at least $300,000 on the sale.

> Business owners can become really narrow in their thinking. They think the only thing they can do is sell their business. We tell them it's important to consider other options as well. (For a list of alternatives, see chapter 26, Fourteen Alternatives to Selling.)
>
> Here are a couple of tales about owners who didn't realize they had another option.

79 SELLING CAN OPEN YOUR EYES

Approximately twenty years ago, I met a man who had a very profitable machine shop. Calvin was operating his shop at about 20% capacity with his equipment. Each piece of equipment was old, but because each piece was dedicated to a specific function for his product, he had lots of spare capacity.

As I walked through the plant with Calvin, I said, "That's strange. You have all this equipment. You must have eighty machines here, but you have only thirty employees to run them."

"We just use this machine here for a couple of hours and

then we use that machine over there for something else. I've got them all set up so I don't have to change tool dyes and jigs as a product moves from one machine to another. And I don't need to buy automatic equipment to make things really efficient. I can't sell any more than I am. I've already got 70% of the market."

"Calvin," I said, "you've got lots of spare capacity. Why are you selling only in Canada? You could be selling in the United States, too."

"Can I do that? How do I do that?" he asked.

He sincerely did not know that he could sell this product in the US, much less how to go about doing so.

We introduced Calvin to government support programs. Three years later Calvin had doubled his revenues and tripled his profits. Somehow he wasn't as interested in selling his business now.

He was just too busy with a very profitable company. He was having the time of his life.

80 THE ANSWER WAS NEXT DOOR

A buyer from Buffalo came to me and wanted to buy an electronics business.

"Really? An electronics business?" I said. "What kind of electronics business?"

Rusty told me he wanted to buy one that manufactured printed circuit boards. Now that's a pretty complex process. And he wanted one that could also do automatic soldering.

As we talked about what his needs were, I learned a lot about his business. And I found out that his business was operating at capacity.

"What kinds of sales do you want this company to do – the one you're thinking about buying?"

"I don't really care, because I've got more business than I'll ever be able to handle."

"Why wouldn't you just go out and buy new equipment?"

"My bank won't lend me any more money."

"Why don't you lease the equipment, then?"

The light bulb went on.

"Leasing? I never thought I could do that."

I gave him the name of a couple of large leasing companies and followed up three weeks later.

"I got my lease," he said, "and I got the equipment that I wanted. Now I've got to add some space for all of this."

He thought that by buying a business he could borrow against the assets of the business. He thought the seller could provide some financing for him.

What he hadn't thought about was that he would be split in two locations. He would have a lot of customers he wouldn't want. He would have employees he might not want. He would have a facility that was incompatible with the facility he had.

As it turned out, there was empty space next door. Rusty extended his lease to include that extra space. He leased the equipment he needed and carried on with his business.

Rusty never did buy a business. Didn't need to.

Chapter *21*

Generation Gaps

An old Chinese proverb says, "He who speaks first, loses." Consequently, I always advise my clients to simply answer any questions put to them by the purchaser during negotiations, without offering any additional information or overtures.

I tell them that when the purchaser is allowed to speak first, we can assess the proposals as they are given to us. It was for this reason that we developed the Robbinex NAP (No Asking Price) Program.

81 *I Put My Foot Down*

I once had a client who had a large manufacturing business. It operated in a 125,000-square-foot facility. Len had a son, Peter, working in the business. We discussed the likelihood that he would take over the business.

Len was adamant that Peter was incapable of running the business. Nor did he have any desire or motivation to run it. Also, Peter lacked the financial capacity to even contemplate acquiring it.

With that information in hand, I went out to find a buyer. I found one in Pittsburgh, forty years old, six foot three, could have passed for Mr. America. He had just sold his own stock-brokerage business for $2 million and wanted something in the manufacturing area.

Skip flew up and I introduced him to our client and showed him around the business. Skip liked the business so he came back and gave us a proposal. I delivered the proposal to Len on Friday around noon.

"Do you mind if I think about it over the weekend?" Len asked, after having looked over the proposal in detail.

"Of course not," I replied. "Let's talk about it on Monday morning."

At 8:15 on Monday morning Len called me.

"I have a problem," he said. "I reviewed the proposal with my family and told them that I was ready to accept it when my son piped up and said that if that was all I wanted for the business, he would buy it."

I reminded Len that he had told me that Peter had no money, so how was he going to pay for it?

"My son has friends from some very wealthy families," Len explained. "They have met and agreed to become my son's partners."

He further instructed me not to lose the buyer from Pittsburgh, but to put him on hold for seven to ten days in order to give his son and the friends an opportunity to put in a proposal.

I met with Peter and his two friends that afternoon. We toured the facility. We reviewed the financial information and the business profile. After that they went away to do their research and to assess their interest in the business.

On Thursday of that same week, one of Peter's friends called me and asked me to meet with him and the others.

They arrived about four in the afternoon. At least the two friends did. Peter was nowhere to be seen. When I inquired as to his whereabouts, I was told that the two friends didn't really want to be in partnership with him. They would rather buy the business themselves.

At this point they presented me with an offer. The offer was for the same price as the fellow from Pittsburgh, except that the down payment was $100,000 higher and the note was $100,000 less. I prepared the documentation and arranged to meet with Len on Monday afternoon.

Len and I sat down in his office about one p.m. on that day. The telephone rang. Len snatched the receiver from the cradle.

"I told you I didn't want to be disturbed," he yelled into the receiver to the receptionist.

There was a long pause. Then he looked at me.

"The phone call's for you," he said and then he threw the phone at me.

I wasn't quick enough to catch it, so it fell and bounced loudly off of the floor.

When I picked up the phone, I found that it was my secretary on the other end of the line.

"This had better be important," I told her.

"Well," she replied, "I have a chap on the phone from Tulsa, Oklahoma. He received the profile from this business about eight months earlier and had passed on it. However, he wants to know if the business is still for sale."

I arranged for the call to be transferred to me and I spoke directly to the fellow, whose name was Kyle. I told Kyle that the business was and wasn't for sale.

There was a pause.

"Well," Kyle said, "make up your mind. Either it's for sale or it isn't for sale."

"As we speak, sir," I told him, "it is for sale. We have two offers on the desk and within an hour it will be sold."

There was another pause.

"Hold on for just a second, please," Kyle said.

I waited for about a minute.

Kyle came back on the line and asked, "Would you wait for twenty-four hours before you make your decision?"

"Why?"

"Well, I'd like to see the business and if it's what I think it is, then I'd like to put in a proposal. Then you can weigh my offer against the other two."

"That'd be fine. But how are you going to get here?"

Kyle told me he would charter a jet and arrive at eight a.m. the following day.

True to his word, Kyle flew into the small community airport, along with five other people: his plant manager, an engineer, his accountant, his sales manager, and an equipment appraiser. We picked them up at the airport and drove them to the business.

We gave them the boardroom. They went through the facility. They split up into teams and they eventually called us into the boardroom just after noon. At this point Kyle made us an offer that was $500,000 higher than the other offers.

When I heard Len take a deep breath to say "sold," I stomped on his foot to stop him.

"Excuse me, fellas," I told Kyle and his companions, "but we're going to have lunch. You're going to have to do better if you want to make this transaction come together."

And off we went. All through lunch Len was moaning and groaning about his foot.

"Sorry about that," I said. "I didn't mean to step on it quite so hard."

By the time we came back from lunch, the price had been raised a further $350,000. Needless to say, I had one happy client, even though I did have to take him to the hospital afterwards.

It turned out that I had broken his small toe.

One generation can differ greatly from the next. Family dynamics come into play. Sometimes the generation that is about to inherit the business may have an inflated idea of their abilities. Sometimes the parents are wearing rose-coloured glasses and can't see the flaws in their offspring.

Either way, when reality arrives, it's always a shock.

82 CREATIVE NON-ACCOUNTING

I received a call from a fellow who was the fourth-generation owner of a family florist business. Martin was looking to transfer the business to his son, Ian, and asked if we help him do that.

It seemed pretty straightforward. So we visited with Martin and his son. Within a week we put together a transaction and everyone agreed to it. Martin and his wife jumped into the family car and drove off to spend the winter in Florida.

In late May of that year I received a call from Martin. "You better get your buns up here Robbins. Ian's lost $80,000 operating the business for the last seven months."

I wondered how could that be. That seven-month period was when the company made all of its profits. Martin had to return from Florida and rescue the business. He had to talk to the bank and put money into the company to pay the payables. In addition, he had to take over the day-to-day operation of the business.

Ian and his wife were devastated by this turn of events. They had withdrawn completely from the family. They even refused Mom and Dad access to the grandchildren. The situation was deteriorating to the point that there was going to be a permanent family rift.

I sat down with Ian to find out what the problem was and

why he had lost all this money. To be quite frank, he did not know. Further probing revealed that he had over-purchased inventory for Christmas and had a large waste factor (nobody buys poinsettias after Christmas).

He had also over-purchased product for Valentine's Day and had another large inventory write-off. He over-purchased for Easter and again for Mother's Day. His wage costs were way out of line, as was his cost of goods sold.

I was told to look for a new buyer. I found a family who was quite anxious to take over the business. They put in a proposal that appeared to be acceptable. I sat down with Martin and his wife, and Ian and his wife, to discuss this offer.

During this process, I asked Ian, "What are you going to do when the business is sold?"

"Oh, I'll probably go to Toronto and find a job as a florist," he said. "I really like this business."

I left that evening perplexed. For a person so passionate about the flower business, how could Ian manage to lose so much money? I then arranged for Ian to meet with a vocational psychologist.

It turned out that Ian was incapable of dealing with the financial end of the business. He could not add or subtract or multiply or divide. He had no concept of numbers. On the other side, Ian had great skills designing flower arrangements and dealing with people.

I went back to Martin and suggested that there might be another alternative to selling the business and would he be game to let me explore it. I then went to a friend of mine who was a chartered accountant. I asked him if his firm would take on the responsibility of being the controller for the company until they could find a proper controller and if they would then supervise the controller.

To make a long story short, an arrangement was negotiated

with Martin. I brought in the accounting firm. They then brought in a bookkeeper. And the accounting firm had a hand in supervising her.

Fifteen years have gone by. Ian and his wife are still operating the florist business. The fifth generation continues.

Many times the children of people who own a business don't want to take it over. For some owners, there is no next generation. The owners are childless, so there is no question of who will inherit the business.

Would-be purchasers often want to get into the business in order to inherit it, but I must tell you it is very rare that a seller will adopt a purchaser and treat them as a surrogate child.

The next tale is one of adoption that happened recently with some clients of mine.

83 CREATING THE NEXT GENERATION

Howard had inherited the business from his father about thirty-five years ago, just after he married Samantha. Unfortunately, he and his wife were unable to have any children and when it came time to consider retiring, they couldn't think of anyone they could transfer the business to.

We provided a value range for this profitable retail business and were asked to try to find a buyer. Within a short time we introduced Samantha and Howard to Amanda, the prospective purchaser. Emotionally, the three were an immediate fit. Financially, not so much.

The selling price was lower than it should have been. Howard and Samantha provided very generous financing terms for Amanda. They wanted the business to survive and continue.

They also wanted Amanda to be successful. They worked diligently to train her in the day-to-day operations of the business and were available for years as coaches and mentors.

They truly did treat her like their own daughter.

Business owners look at succession planning as a simple and natural progression. For decades, the unspoken understanding is that the next generation will inherit the business. After all, *they* inherited this legacy from their folks and ran it successfully, didn't they?

Even though nothing is said, it is assumed that the offspring will automatically step in and carry on in the business.

84 THEIR THREE SONS

I reviewed a family operation in which three brothers were discussing what to do with the business. Their father had died recently, leaving it to his sons.

Bert, sixty four years old had just been visited by the dreaded C word. He had had his prostate removed. Randy, fifty-two years old, had just experienced a spike in his stress level with the addition of a shunt in his major artery after a mild heart attack. And Ellis, forty-one years old, had been rushed to the hospital with chest pains that were subsequently attributed to stress. He was now taking medication for it.

The business was profitable and had been valued at $8 million. The business had been in the family for three generations. There was a perceived obligation that it needed to be passed on to the fourth generation.

I had our psychologist interview each member of the third generation.

Interviews and testing of the three brothers revealed that Bert, the eldest, was in great financial shape. He could retire whenever he wanted. But his role in the business was such that he felt he had a duty to the others and couldn't just set a date and leave. Bert's wife wanted him out now because of his problems with cancer.

Randy wanted to stay because he really enjoyed the work. In his mind, he hadn't really accumulated enough to retire.

Ellis, the youngest, had recently divorced. He had given a huge percentage of his net worth to his ex-wife and was in no position to think about retirement. He had unique technical skills and knowledge but no business or sales/marketing skills to take over the business.

A financial planner was brought in to review each brother's personal situation, coupled with the psychologist's recommendations. In the end it was decided that the business should be sold. Each brother would net approximately $2.2 million after taxes from the sale. A family trust was created to pass the wealth on to their children.

Bert would work with the purchaser for three months and invest his net proceeds from the sale.

Randy would stay on as president and would retain about 10% equity in the company. His net proceeds of the portion he sold would be invested for his future retirement.

Ellis had indicated his strong desire to become a commercial pilot. He invested his share from the sale into a universal life insurance policy; borrowed $1 million against the policy; and invested in a small private cargo airline.

Each of the brothers had his own personal goals and objectives. They had put shelved them to please their father. Dad had wanted to fulfill the legacy of carrying on the family business and move it to the fourth generation.

Even though Dad had passed on, Mom wholly endorsed the final decision of selling the business rather than keeping it with the hope that the fourth generation would one day take over ... maybe.

Chapter *22*

Qualifying Buyers

Buyers come in all sizes and shapes. And we've learned over the years that for almost every business we take to market, we generally wind up touching at least 200 potential buyers.

The largest number of buyers we touched on in one business before we sold it was 879. And the smallest has been 1. For the most part, the number is somewhere between 150 and 250 buyers for every business that we find and complete a transaction on.

It's really important to take the time to qualify the person who's looking to buy your business. You need to qualify them under what we call The Three Ms. They need to have the money. They need to have management skills. And they need to be properly motivated.

"Wait a minute," you say. "What do you mean by motivated?"

Here's a tale that's an excellent example of motivation … or the lack of it.

85 STILL LOOKING

Many years ago I worked on a partnership between two brothers. Gerry was fifty-one and his younger brother, Riley, was forty-five. The father had passed away, leaving each of them with 50% of the company. It was a fairly large company.

Revenue was about $35 million a year. Gerry and Riley worked all their lives in the company and within a very short period of time, their own sons were working in it as well.

And then the friction began between the cousins. Of course, the uncles got involved in the conflict, too. Who was going to run the company? Who was going to do this or that? The fighting became fierce.

The brothers' lawyer suggested they bring us in to see if we could come up with a resolution.

After spending some time with our psychologist, it became obvious who should keep the business and who should leave. The exiting partner, Gerry, left with $2.5 million after tax. That was in October.

Gerry called me in January and said, "You know what? This not having a business sucks. I had to buy postage stamps for the first time in my life to send out Christmas cards. I need to buy a business. What have you got for sale?"

I knew Gerry had $2.5 million to spend and had run a large distribution company doing sales of about $35 million. That made him highly qualified to run certain types of businesses.

I happened to have a business available in Mississauga, which was approximately thirty miles from where Gerry lived. Unfortunately, that part of Mississauga is heavily traversed in the morning.

Gerry's first comment was, "Why would I want to buy a business in Mississauga? Who wants to travel in all that traffic every day?"

"Well, Gerry, you can time-shift,' I said. You can go in early in the morning and come home early in the afternoon. You can go in late in the morning and come home early in the evening, after the traffic dissipates."

"Well, yeah, maybe you got a point," he said. "Let's go have a look at this."

So we had a look at the business. Gerry was quite excited about the business model itself. We went to a preliminary meeting with the client about six o'clock one evening after all the employees had left. Generally these meetings and a walk through a business takes about ninety minutes.

When we finally parted at midnight, the dynamics and the enthusiasm between the buyer and the seller told me I had a buyer who wanted to buy a business.

I phoned Gerry the next morning and said, "Great. Let's get together and put an offer in on this business."

"No way I'm going to buy a business in Mississauga. The traffic's terrible. What else have you got for sale?"

"As it turns out, I do have a business for sale," I said. "It's closer to where you live, but it's not as big and it doesn't make as much money. And it doesn't have the same potential."

"Well, let's have a look at it," Gerry said.

So we visited this business. We had the business profiles and we went down to visit the client about five-thirty in the evening. We stayed there until eight-thirty. Gerry was really excited about this business, too.

I called Gerry the next morning and said we should put in an offer.

"No, no, no, no. This business isn't as good as the one in Mississauga."

"Great. Then let's buy the one in Mississauga."

"No, no, no. I'm not driving in all that traffic. What else do you have for sale?"

I thought about it for thirty seconds and said, "Gerry, I don't have anything for sale that will meet your needs at this point in time. But I will certainly keep you in mind for the future."

As time went on, I started receiving calls from real estate brokers, bankers, lawyers, accountants, inquiring if I had any businesses for sale because they had a client with $2.5 million who wanted to buy a business.

"Oh, you must be talking to Gerry," I would say.

"How did you know?" they would ask.

"Because he's talking to everybody in the city."

About two years later, I was in a small community meeting with a potential client who had really left it too long. Wesley was going broke. A receiver had been appointed. A trustee was on the premises. So was a bailiff. Everybody was fighting for the assets when I arrived.

I spoke to Wesley for about fifteen minutes and said, "You know, it's too late. I can't really help you. If you had called me in six months earlier, I might have been able to. But there's not much I can do for you today. I'm sorry."

"Well, I know, but I was sort of hoping," he said. "But I've got one last chance. I've got an investor. I have someone who indicated he might be willing to invest."

"Wonderful! Good luck to you," I said.

So Wesley walked me to the front door. And who was sitting in the lobby? Gerry! I shook Gerry's hand vigorously and told him it was good to see him.

I turned to Wesley and said, "If Gerry wants to put the money up, I can tell you that he's got it. No question about that."

So I left.

The following day I bumped into Gerry on our way out of the Rotary club.

"Hey, what did you think about that business yesterday?" I asked him.

"Oh, that was a terrible business. But I haven't got time to talk about it now," he said. "I have an appointment at the stationery store."

And I said, "O-k-a-a-y…"

I'd never heard of anybody making an appointment at the stationery store before.

"Why would you make an appointment there?"

"Oh, I have five filing cabinets at home and they are all made by a manufacturer that went out of business and I need a couple more. They may have two of these things and I've got them on hold. I need to make sure that they're the same as the filing cabinets I've got at home."

That sort of made sense, but then I thought, "Gerry is still without a business. Why does he have five filing cabinets and now need two more?"

"Gerry, what's in the filing cabinets?"

"Oh, Doug, I'm working on my two hundred and sixty-eighth deal," he said.

Gerry wasn't really a motivated buyer. He was busy clipping coupons from the $2.5 million he had invested. He was just having a good time looking at all kinds of businesses.

Unfortunately for Gerry, his wife left him. Now he has $1.25 million to invest and he's still looking. Anybody want his telephone number?

> As the seller of a business, it's important for you to know beyond The Three Ms exactly who the buyer is. What type of person are you selling to? Qualifying a buyer for integrity and confidentiality is very important.
>
> This next tale is a good illustration of the unethical buyer.

86 RUNNING INTERFERENCE

Dylan owned a manufacturing firm located in a small southwestern Ontario city. Sam came along and expressed an interest in buying the business. Sam signed a Confidentiality

Agreement and gave it to Dylan, which, when I read it, was of no value. It did not protect Dylan in any way.

Sam went through the business and learned all about it. He discovered our client had a major customer who represented about 50% of his revenue – about $5.5 million.

Sam then went directly to that customer and said, "Look, Dylan is about to go broke and you should really give me all the business or you're going to find your shelves empty."

So the major customer cancelled the orders with Dylan and went with the competitor.

Fortunately, I happened to be on the scene when that happened. Dylan and I went down to meet the customer directly.

"You need to know what happened," I said. "It's wrong. Sam approached us and indicated that he wanted to buy the business. And we said anything is for sale if the price is right. Here's the Confidentiality Agreement that Sam signed. Unfortunately it isn't valid. But, quite frankly, we are going to sue him anyway for interfering with our customer and you are probably going to get dragged into the lawsuit. I expect it would be easier if you were just to stop buying from this nasty guy and come back with us."

And that's what happened.

> It is so important to know who you are dealing with; how much money the purchaser has; and how the deal is going to be financed.

87 NOTHING TO HIDE

Roy is a fellow in Toronto who owned a fairly large direct-to-consumer business with a high profile in the community. Very profitable. He called us up one day and asked me to come for a visit. He was ready to sell his business.

As we talked to him, we discovered that he had been trying

to complete a transaction to sell the business for eighteen months. And he had a Letter of Intent in place from a chap named Bruce, but it was subject to financing. He was happy with the terms and conditions in Bruce's Letter of Intent, but Bruce couldn't get it financed.

As we started to investigate, we found that Bruce had no money of his own. And while the people he was looking to finance with were all interested in financing the business, they didn't particularly care for his business acumen or his financial contribution insofar as equity was concerned.

Pretty soon virtually everybody in the business community within a fifty-mile radius of Roy's business knew it was for sale. It also seemed that many folks inside and outside the financing world knew about it as well. Everybody knew about the details, too. They knew what the company's revenues were; what its profits were; how many employees it had, and its gross margins. I mean, the whole thing was just an open book.

Roy was very fortunate that none of his key people left. Had it been a different kind of business, he could have lost all of his staff, key customers, and key suppliers.

After nineteen months, Bruce finally put a group of investors together who ultimately helped him obtain the necessary financing.

Industrial espionage, stealing trade secrets, sounds like something out of a comic book. It's not comical at all. It's very real. Although little attention is given to it, this kind of espionage is of immense proportions and growing every day.

In this next tale, the name of the process, the trade secret, has been changed considerably in order to avoid … well, you'll see.

88 REVEALING SECRETS

I had a client whose company manufactured a product that was very specific to the end-customer use. We will call the process "fusion."

Normally fusion was a long and laborious process with many steps to it. It took three to four days before everything was dry and ready to be shipped to the customer. It was used by cosmetic companies. Very complicated stuff.

Well, Nelson had come up with a way of condensing the time involved while still producing a first-class product. His customers and competitors tried but were unable to duplicate his process.

I said to Nelson, "Look, you should keep this highly confidential. Nobody should be allowed in the back of your plant until they've bought the business. It's highly confidential. It's proprietary. It's secretive, like the Coca-Cola recipe. It's not patented, but nobody knows what it is or how to do it."

Nelson agreed.

I worked with him for about three months. He called me up one day and said, "Doug, I think I've got a problem."

"What's your problem?"

"Well, my major customer's vice president of sales was over to see me. And we went out for lunch. We each had a bottle of wine."

"Man, that's a lot of wine," I said. "I hope you didn't drive back."

"No. We got into a cab and went back to the office. But I gave the guy a tour and we stopped at my fusion machine. He said, 'Oh, that's how you do it! I've often wondered how you do that.' And he looked at the machine very closely."

Four weeks later Nelson's major customer chartered a 747 and flew in a machine from Germany to duplicate the process.

Nelson's sales dropped 60%.

You never know when someone is going to ask if your business is for sale. It doesn't happen often, but it's another good reason to be prepared to sell.

This next tale is about how some people can be in the right place at just the right time.

89 TAKE THE MONEY AND RUN

We had just been retained to assess a business a number of years ago when a nearby competitor unexpectedly came knocking on our door. The competitor had a proposal to purchase Harvey's business for $5 million.

At this point, we hadn't established a value range. So we quickly accelerated that process. To everyone's surprise, traditional valuation methods proposed a range of between $3.5 million and $4 million.

When negotiations concluded, $6.5 million was paid for Harvey's business.

Motivation and competence are a great recipe for success. However, lack of motivation and incompetence are a recipe for disaster.

90 THERE'S ALWAYS TOMORROW

The buyer, Nolan, was a schoolteacher who ran the technical department of a high school. His father had passed away, leaving him with $1 million. Nolan decided that he no longer wanted to be a teacher; he wanted to be in the hardware business.

I didn't have any hardware stores for sale at the time, but I did have a farm implement dealership.

"That's exciting! I'm a gentleman farmer. I have fifteen acres and I have tractors and plows and shears and lawnmowers and all that kind of stuff. Boy, this would be wonderful."

So we went up and visited with the seller, Sid. At the end of the day, Nolan put in an offer and the offer was accepted. One of the conditions was that Sid would stay in the business for ninety to one hundred and twenty days to help Nolan learn the business.

About ninety days later I got a call from Sid.

"Doug, you'd better come up here," he said. "We've got a real problem with Nolan."

"Sure, but what's the problem?"

"He's not learning and he doesn't want to learn how to run the business. I'm still running it."

"Well, that sounds like a real problem."

"Yeah, I'd like to get out of here in the next thirty days," Sid said. "I've got my money, but I hate to see the guy go broke."

So I drove up a couple of days later. When I pulled into the dealership, what did I see but Nolan in coveralls painting a sign pole at the front of the building.

"Why are you painting that?" I said. "You've got all kinds of people you could hire at minimum wage to paint for you."

"Oh well, Doug, I enjoy it," he said. "It's kind of fun. It's relaxing and there's no pressure here."

"Yeah, but Nolan, you've got to run the business."

"Oh well," he said. "I'll get to that sooner or later."

I went in and talked to Sid. He was busy dealing with customers on the phone, dealing with employees, and dealing with suppliers. He was working way too hard. We sat down a few minutes later and chatted.

"You know, the guy still doesn't even know who to order product from," Sid told me. "He doesn't know who his best customers are. He hasn't taken any interest in the business. The employees all think he's a jerk. I just don't know what to do."

I went back out and tried to convince Nolan that he had to do something.

"Yeah, Doug, I'll get started tomorrow," he said.

To make a long story short, tomorrow never did come. About nine months later Nolan went bankrupt. He lost everything, including his farm and his father's money.

Nolan sued everybody: his lawyer, his accountant, his banker. He sued the seller. He sued the seller's accountant and the seller's lawyer and he sued us.

Everybody had to spend a lot of money on legal fees, but at the end of the day, the judge threw Nolan's claim out.

Chapter *23*

Get Me Outta Here

A family unit can be very powerful. The heirs or heiresses to the family business may give up their dreams in order to fulfill family expectations of them. Rather than follow their passion, they succumb to family pressures.

To some heirs and heiresses, it may not seem worthwhile to even attempt to climb out of that family-made trench.

91 THOSE WHO CAN DO, TEACH

Mark was the heir apparent of the family business. He was the only child. Because the business had been so successful, Mark had been allowed to pursue his own dreams. He had become a teacher.

Mark loved teaching. He loved the subjects he taught. He liked the students. He liked everything about his role as a teacher. And even though he would make an awful lot more money running the business, his preference was clearly to keep teaching.

Out of family loyalty, however, he decided to take on the business. He had a strong sense of obligation. He felt he owed his parents. So he sacrificed his own dreams and interests and gave up his career as a teacher.

Mark ran the family business for many years. One day about eleven years later, he phoned me.

"Dad has passed on," he said. "Look, I want to sell this business. I never wanted to be in the business. I only took it over because Dad wanted me to and now I want out. Can you help me get out of this?"

"Yes," I said, and I did.

Mark is now back doing what he loves ... teaching.

> Well-intentioned business owners are so busy running their businesses they sometimes turn around and say, "Hey, how did all this happen? I need to get out of this mess."

> This next tale is a great example of the complexity of family-run businesses. It's often not just one thing that needs fixing.

92 OUT OF THE SHADOWS

Approximately eighteen years ago I was approached by Graham, who wanted to know if I could put a value on his business. Of course I said yes.

While our Comprehensive Business Analysis was under way, I learned the business had undertaken a significant expansion about three years earlier. The cost of the expansion was $3 million.

The completion of the project was currently running behind schedule. It was one year late and it would be another six months before the new facility would be in production. Sales were $6 million. One customer represented 65% of total sales.

The company recorded a loss of approximately $400,000 that year and $250,000 in the previous year. Most of these losses were incurred as a direct result of interest costs on the money borrowed for capital for the expansion program and annual donations of $300,000. And still Graham would not able to make use of the efficiencies that the new plant would create for at least six to eight months until it was operational.

Early on in the process I learned that Graham's banker was uncomfortable. He had threatened to call in the company's loans. In fact, the bank had found a purchaser and was insisting that Graham sell the business to the purchaser for an amount Graham felt was low. This turned out to be why Graham had us come in and value the business. It turned out our value was more than two times the offer from the bank's client.

I then made an appointment with the banker to discuss his concerns. I learned that he had lost confidence in Graham. He felt that at the age of seventy-three Graham was no longer capable of successfully managing the company. He expressed concern about the 65% customer and he made a comment that the bank was quite capable of choosing its own charities.

It turned out that a number of years ago, Graham had pledged $3 million to his church congregation in order to build a new church and that his annual donation came to $300,000.

I met with the major customer. I quickly learned that this customer, whose sales were $150 million a year, could be put out of business or seriously compromised by our client if he failed to deliver the $4 million of product the customer purchased each year. I then negotiated an evergreen contract with the customer, requiring two years' notice of cancellation with provisions built into the contract for increases in labour and material costs.

Next, I visited the minister of Graham's church. He told me the congregation had more than doubled in size since the church was constructed. The church no longer relied on Graham's pledge to meet its obligations and sustain the mortgage payments.

I advised Graham to purchase an insurance policy from which, on his passing, the church would receive $2 million. The premiums on the policy were fairly expensive, about $30,000 a year, but a lot less than $300,000.

As for his management team, I learned he had his three children working in the business. Turns out they were working in the shadow of their father. They were all quite capable in their own right. Collectively they formed a very competent business team that Graham ruled with an iron fist. Nothing happened that he didn't approve. Quite frankly, this was a significant part of the reason that the business expansion was behind schedule.

Several recommendations were made and followed. Eighteen years later the company's sales were $30 million with pre-tax profits of $4.5 million per year.

Graham has retired from the business, and is alive and well.

> When it comes to digging businesses out of self-made trenches, there is nothing quite like an advisory board. Here's a tale of how a team of experts helped a company.

93 THE VALUE OF FULL DISCLOSURE

Donny and Erica, a husband and wife team, approached us a number of years ago to sell their company. The company was not performing very well. It had an EBITDA of $300,000. After depreciation it showed a small operating loss. The company was undercapitalized. The bank loan was operating at its peak almost constantly. Book value of the company was $1 million. The bank loan was $2.5 million. The accounts receivable was $2 million. Inventory was showing at $1.5 million.

We went through a phase one Analysis and noted the industry standard for this type of business had an EBITDA of 10%. If this company was operating at 10% it would make the business worth a great deal more money than the $1.5 million at which we had set the value.

I encouraged Donny and Erica to hire a chief executive

officer to help them operate the business. I explained that they would probably have to pay this person $120,000 a year plus bonuses of up to $30,000 if he or she achieved goals and objectives that were set out.

They asked me where they could find such a person. I referred them to three different headhunters.

After about five weeks, Donny called back and said, "Look, we don't like any of these head hunters we met. And we don't like any of the people they have sent around to see us. Erica and I would like to hire you as our CEO."

I was honoured but explained to them that I was already the CEO of a company, one that I already owned, and I really didn't have time to be two CEOs.

"No, no!" Donny said. "You don't understand. You have a great team of people. Perhaps you can put together a team or committee that can help us with our problems."

I told him I would think about it and get back to him in a couple of days. I remembered that I knew a chap, Les, from our Rotary club who had recently retired – a former vice president of one of the national banks. I respected this fellow's ability and integrity. He had taken an early retirement.

"Les, would you be interested in a part-time assignment?" I asked him. "Maybe three days a week? The assignment may last six to eight months, maybe even a year."

Les pondered it for a while. We agreed on terms and conditions. Next I pulled one of our accountants from Robbinex to work a day a week with the client and I spent half a day a week myself with the team.

Within thirty-five days we discovered that there were significant errors in the accounting procedures. Inventory was overstated. Receivables were overstated. Accounts payable were understated. The result? There was no book value in the company.

We pointed out to Donny and Erica that this, in effect, was fraudulent as far as their bank would be concerned. We had to talk to their bank about it.

Donny absolutely refused us permission to talk to the bank. So we quit. We didn't feel we could carry on a charade with the bank and maintain our reputation.

"You can't quit!" Donny said. "What do I tell the bank?"

My response was, "Have the banker call me and I will tell him why I quit."

The air was blue with swearing for a few minutes after that. Donny reluctantly agreed that we could go in and sit down with the banker.

We met with the banker a couple of days later. The colour drained from his face when I explained the problem and the accounting error. We assured him that the company was operating at a break-even or a small profit, and that we were in there providing consulting services on a daily basis.

We also agreed to provide a monitoring function for the bank. We reported to the bank every week on receivables, payables, inventory levels, and orders on hand.

The retired banker mercilessly whipped the company into shape. He had an MBA and he really meant business – all the time. Within six months the company was operating at an annualized EBITDA of about $600,000. Within nine months its annualized EBITDA was $1.5 million, or 15%.

Lo and behold, someone came along and offered Donny and Erica $7 million for the business. The transaction closed a couple of months later.

> Due diligence is like looking through a magnifying glass at every facet of a company's operation. Every area is analyzed and evaluated. Competent intermediaries initiate this process before the business is taken to

market, because it will help their clients get the best price possible, without surprises.

Some clients are in too much of a rush to sell. Interestingly, even accountants may fail to listen to professional advice.

94 *"Just Get Me Out!"*

I received a call from a Rotarian in a nearby city who wanted to know what he should do with a business he had just inherited. Ray was an accountant. He had no experience operating a business. The business he had inherited had revenues of $12 million. It employed sixty-five members of the steelworkers union. In addition, there were six folks in the office.

Ray's father had passed away suddenly and Ray had inherited the business. His Dad had left no contingency plans for the operation or sale.

Ray had a thriving public practice. He had no desire to give it up. So he had made arrangements to manage the business (sort of) for the next ninety to a hundred and twenty days and wanted it sold quickly.

In touring the business, I noted that the company was operating at capacity and was turning away a significant amount of business. The tour revealed an obvious bottleneck at a production turntable. I commented that if the bottleneck could be eliminated, sales would increase; profits would rise; and the value would increase substantially.

Ray responded in a surly manner.

"What part of 'quick' don't you understand? I don't want to be here. I don't want to run this business. Just get me out!"

Within about five months we found a buyer who paid a fair price for the company. The deal closed about six weeks later. The buyer had also noticed the bottleneck. He corrected it, at a cost of about $100,000. This improvement increased the revenues by $6 million in the first year of ownership and made him an extra $1 million in operating profit.

Being too anxious to sell the business cost Ray somewhere in the vicinity of $3 million to $4 million in the selling price.

Chapter *24*

Have an Exit Strategy

A professional practice is a business, just like any other, and partnerships are prone to fail. The cost of setting up the correct structure for operating and ultimately terminating the partnership is relatively inexpensive compared with the cost of unraveling a relationship that no longer meets the original needs, not to mention the emotional cost.

In a sense, terminating a business partnership is rather like a divorce.

Without a prenuptial agreement, it can become very messy indeed.

95 SILENT PARTNERS

I had lunch recently with an associate of mine who is contemplating retiring. Vincent is sixty-two and has an interest in a small insurance business. Last year he took eleven weeks of vacation and is planning on taking twelve to fifteen weeks this year. Over lunch he told me his conscience was bothering him. He felt he was not being fair to his partners by taking so much vacation time.

However, Vincent indicated that he had no intention of cutting back on vacations. He wanted to continue to take a great deal of time off in the years ahead. He went on to say that he really enjoyed the business. He didn't want to retire totally.

I asked him what he liked and disliked about the business. We talked about his relationship with his partners. He asked what I thought he should do based on my years of experience as a business broker.

"Each person has a capacity for work," I told him. "Let's call that capacity a hundred units. As we get older, our capacity to work reduces. So the most important thing we can do is ensure that we're not operating beyond our capacity at any point in time.

"Ideally," I added, "we should work at between 80% and 90% of our capacity. This leaves us with a capacity to handle the unexpected and extraordinary. Therefore, if in our prime we can do a hundred units of work, historically then as we get older we may find we can only do eighty units of work. Therefore we should reduce the commitment to the total number of units."

"This makes a lot of sense to me," Vincent said.

"We then need to look at the units themselves. Let us presume that each unit has five components of work in total. And upon further examination we discover that we like doing two of the components and don't really care about doing the other three components."

I told Vincent that when we're younger, our capacity for work is higher. We did the three components of work we didn't like to do because they had to be done. As we grew older, we need to be more selective about the work we do.

"We look around to see if perhaps we can delegate those three components of work that we don't enjoy to someone else."

The discussion turned to his partnership arrangement. I was surprised to learn that not only was there no written partnership agreement, but there was nothing *at all* in writing to summarize their working relationship.

Each of the partners had their own book of business in

addition to a shared book of business. They each paid their proportionate share of expenses. Each partner made a different amount of money. And each partner had a different sense of the value that should be used to calculate their own book of business.

Indeed, they had not even made provisions for the untimely demise of one of the partners. Remember, these partners sold life insurance and financial planning to their clients. Talk about the shoemaker not making shoes for his own family.

This lack of value consensus could, at some point in the future, prove explosive.

Our recommendations were quite straightforward:

- summarize the current operating arrangements between the three partners
- discuss changes in the operating agreements in order to compensate for extended time off being contemplated by the senior partner
- organize an independent valuation of each of the practices and the shared practice
- establish a buy-sell agreement between the three partners, taking into consideration the financial capability of the individual partners to pay
- arrange sufficient life insurance to cover the values determined by the valuations
- consider arranging long-term lump sum income disability coverage
- do it now
- set reasonable time lines to complete each of the above
- retain competent professionals to complete the work in a timely manner.

Vincent became one of our clients. So did his two partners.

wis Carroll, author of *Alice in Wonderland*, said, "If don't know where you are going, any road will take u there."

A shareholders' agreement can provide business partners with a road map that shows where they started, where they are now, and where they're going. The trick is to follow the road map.

It isn't uncommon for several years to go by before a business is sold. When we turn on the selling process – from the time the client says, "Let's sell" – it takes us about sixty days to get the client's business ready for market, because there is a lot of research and packaging to be done. And when we turn it on, it usually takes three to six to nine months to find the buyer and two to four months to close the transaction once the buyer is found.

We did a study recently and found it was averaging about thirty-eight months to go from the client's first call until the cheque was in the bank.

Usually a business owner will arrange a meeting to discuss the selling process or perhaps they will attend a workshop. Then anywhere from two weeks to four years later they will decide to "discover what it's really worth" and learn about "alternatives." That process should take about sixty days but many clients are too busy to provide the necessary information needed to complete the assignment. So, a period of four to six months is not uncommon to complete the first phase. Oftentimes the client will stop at this point to implement value enhancement recommendations.

Some clients take a little more time and some take a little less. One of the shortest transactions I was ever involved in took nine months.

96 A Nine-Month Gestation

Isaac, the owner of a car dealership in Chicago, was eighty-two years old. He had 80% of the shares. He also had a partner, Manny, who was sixty-five.

When he was just thirty, Isaac bought the business with five partners. They had a shareholders' agreement back then. When a partner reached sixty-five, the other partners were supposed to buy him out. But for some reason, when Isaac reached sixty-five nothing happened. Anyway, he was one of the two partners left. So he and Manny were running the business.

Manny walks in and says to Isaac, "Well, I'm sixty-five now. I'm retiring. Where's my cheque?"

Isaac bought him out.

It was really funny. Isaac didn't even know the names of the different models of cars, much less the features of each model. We went out to lunch one day in one of his cars and I said, "Which model is this that you're driving?"

"I don't know," he said. "I just turn the key and drive it."

Sales of the dealership had dropped from five hundred new models a year to fewer than a hundred. So Isaac wasn't in the manufacturer's good books either.

We did our work and found a buyer and sold it very quickly. It still took a long time to go through all the gyrations and legal problems and various issues. There was an old franchisee agreement. There were environmental issues as well. The new franchisee had to be approved by the manufacturer.

Still, this was a fast transaction. I believe that we started on January 15 and closed on October 15.

Here's another tale from the trenches. It illustrates the great importance of an exit strategy.

97 THE ELEPHANT IN THE ROOM

It was time for Ned to retire from the family business. But Ned didn't have an exit strategy, so he came to us. He and his wife, Joanne, had three children – two sons and a daughter. All three siblings were married. All three worked in the business with Mom and Dad. It was a profitable business. Revenue was $8 million per year.

Our vocational psychologist interviewed each member of the family – father, mother, the three children, and each of their spouses.

Joanne was a delightful woman who referred to the business as "the monster." She had made a rule that at family gatherings and holidays, no one was to talk about the business. This was really hard to do because everyone was involved in it.

Joanne wanted the business sold. In assessing the family members, we discovered that the daughter and the son-in-law, who were a number of years older than the sons, had done well. They had been well paid by the success of the business and were at a point in their lives where they weren't that interested in owning it or even running it. In fact, they were really kind of looking forward to retirement themselves. They had a nice nest egg and felt they could retire.

Wally, the elder son, described his job as basically making sure that the vehicles used in the business were washed. He ran the car wash, which was part of the business. He had never read a financial statement. He had never been in any kind of a managerial role. He knew almost nothing about the workings of the business. He definitely wasn't a candidate for taking over the management.

Frank, the younger son, was the head of a small division of the company. It was similar to a customer service business. This division lost money every year, mainly because they charged for a product that they distributed but not for a portion of their service.

"What do you like most about your job?" I asked Frank.

He said he liked to go out on calls to deliver this product. He was often invited in to have tea. That was his favourite part of the job. Frank wasn't really interested in managing anything. And he had very little knowledge about how to run the other aspects of the business.

All of these members of the family were in the business and receiving salaries far and above what they could have demanded in a competitive environment. All of them were well off financially.

Dad was the only one fit to run the business. If somebody bought the business, they wouldn't keep the siblings.

This family was in distress. They didn't have any kind of an exit strategy.

The vocational psychologist and I got the whole family together. We talked about "the elephant in the room." We suggested that they schedule a family meeting to discuss all of this, including the psychologist's reports and evaluations.

At that meeting I laid it out for them.

"Basically, the dilemma is this. Ned, you can't transfer this business to your children. There's no one who is either capable or willing enough to take it on. If you sell it, Wally and Frank and their families are going to be seriously affected. They won't have jobs. At the very least, they'll have to take about a two-third cut in salary. If you keep running it, Ned, at some point you will no longer be capable of doing it. So, what do you want to do as a family?"

A very interesting discussion took place. Basically what they ended up saying was, "We'll do what Dad wants to do."

"I don't want to create any problems for my children, so I'll just keep running it," Ned said.

That's what they came up with.

Unfortunately, they had put themselves in a very difficult position. There weren't too many good options as far as this family was concerned.

The business probably could have been sold for a nice sum of money. Ned and Joanne would have been pretty well off. The older sister and her husband would have been okay, but the two younger boys – and they weren't that young; Frank and Wally were pushing forty – would have been in trouble. They didn't know how to run the business. They wouldn't have been able to get jobs anywhere else that paid them anything like what they were making. They would be fired if someone else came in. Or they would have to take a significant cut in pay.

Another possibility for Ned would have been to devote some time and energy into bringing Frank up to snuff. However, to get him into a position to manage the business would take years at best.

At the end of the day, it was agreed that a professional manager would be hired to operate the business.

> The best time to think about selling your business is when you don't have to sell it at all. If you do your thinking and planning ahead of time, you can develop a good exit strategy and the business can be sold successfully when the time comes. If a crisis happens, you are prepared.

Chapter 25

Selling ... Successfully

It's worth repeating: "Sell your business when you don't have to!" If you *have* to sell your business for a particular reason – health (illness or aging), divorce (this includes spouses *and* common-law partners), financial difficulties – you may not get the full financial value of your company.

And to sell your business successfully, you need professional assistance. You need to trust these professionals. They have to have a proven record of experience, integrity, and respect for others. They need to know the complexities of buying and selling businesses.

There is no need to wait until the decades fly by to seek out these life-altering decisions. Just knowing what to do and how to do it will give any business owner peace of mind.

The next tale is a great example of how a team of specialists can provide positive solutions to challenging problems.

98 OF THREE MINDS ABOUT SELLING

I was called into the midst of a partnership dispute between two brothers and a boyhood friend. All three had started a business together in the late seventies with a total investment of about $15,000. They started by selling franchises.

When I met them sales were running at about $30 million.

They had about a hundred and fifty stores in Canada and the US, generating about $1 million of profit after paying each of them $250,000 a year in wages.

But Edgar, Alex, and Reese had been fighting for a number of years. Two of them would gang up and fire the third. Then he'd hire a lawyer and get a court order to get his job back. Then he'd buddy up with one of the other partners and go after the third. It was a mish-mash and now was at the point where none of them would meet with one another or talk to one another without their lawyer present. Legal fees were running $200,000 a year and the business was languishing, to say the least.

I met with the three partners and the only thing we could agree on was that the business ought to be valued. They enlisted an accountant to work with me on the valuation. We came up with a value range of $6.5 to $6.8 million.

We presented this to the three partners.

"Smack on," Edgar said.

"Man, that's way more than I thought," Alex said.

"There's no bloody way! It's worth a lot more than you've come up with," Reese said.

Well at least they were consistent.

I provided each of the partners with a list of business appraisers and an extra copy of my valuation report. I asked them to select an appraiser from the list and send him a cheque for $500 plus the valuation report for a second opinion on our valuation.

Each partner did so. All three appraisers came back saying they agreed with the range we had put on the business.

Then I started the negotiations. Who was going to buy and who was going to sell? After many months, I finally convinced Alex and Reese to buy out Edgar. But there was still an obstacle.

Edgar was prepared to sell to Alex and Reese at a purchase

price of $2.5 million, but his accountant told him he would need to pay $900,000 in income tax for the sale of his third to the other two partners. Of course, Edgar didn't want to pay that much in taxes.

Tax specialists were brought in. They happened to be part of a law firm in which all the senior members were also accountants. They did nothing but tax-structuring transactions. They were able to restructure the transaction so Edgar still received his $2.5 million but paid only $80,000 in income tax. Edgar was elated.

The moral of the story: There's power in a second opinion.

> Peter Drucker is quoted as saying, "The buyer never buys what the seller is selling."
>
> You really need to know what your buyer's buying before you try to sell him a business. You need to take time to find out the buyer's needs, his wants, his problems, his issues, his fears, and his nightmares. When you understand who that buyer is and where he's coming from, you can position yourself to meet his needs.
>
> And if you meet his needs, you can sell your business for a good price.

99 PERCEPTION IS EVERYTHING

We were called in one day to look at a company that was in the specialized trucking business. Milt had forty trucks and substantial customers. He was thirty-seven or thirty-eight years old and looked like he was fifty. And as I got to know him, I found out that he worked roughly eighteen hours a day, six and a half days a week.

Milt said to me, "I've just gotta get out of this business. Many times I sleep in the truck and get up in the morning and just keep on going."

I visited his business and was impressed with what I saw.

Many of the details we needed – financial information, a list of all the equipment, details about the contracts – were there.

Milt called me one morning.

"Doug, I've got an offer coming in. I'm going to need an accountant and a lawyer and you. I assume you'll help me with this offer."

"Absolutely."

I arranged for an accountant and a lawyer and the three of us went to meet with Milt. Then Milt and I went to meet the buyer. The buyer made an opening offer of $8 million.

Milt was about to say yes but I gave him a nudge with my elbow and said, "We'll get back to you in a couple of days, if that's okay with you."

It was.

Once Milt and I were back in the car I said, "Milt, you're not telling me everything I need to know."

"What do you mean?"

"Our valuator just said $4 million to $4.5 million. That buyer knows something about this business that I don't know and you are going to tell me everything I need to know."

So we went back to my office. We put him on the grill for twelve hours, from eleven in the morning to eleven at night We went back up to his place at eight the next morning with a full team of people and we were there until ten that night. Yet we still couldn't find anything indicating that his business was worth $8 million.

I told my team this called for drastic action.

"What's that?" they asked.

"The LL program," I replied. "Yes, the Liquid Lunch."

So I called the buyer and asked him to meet me at the martini bar about one o'clock to grab a sandwich.

I went to the martini bar and I was deliberately twenty minutes late. I had called and said, "I'm tied up and I'm going to be a few minutes late." I wanted him to be hungry.

So we went in and ordered double martinis. We had a small sandwich and then another double martini. And then a third double martini. We left at about 3:30.

I called taxis for the two of us because neither of us was in any shape to drive. A little while later I called the client.

"Milt, from this point forward until we finish negotiating, your plant is quarantined. Nobody is allowed in your building without my express written permission. That includes suppliers, customers, government inspectors, repairmen, electricians – nobody comes into that plant."

"Why?"

"This buyer thinks you've got a secret process in that plant and he's prepared to pay a lot more than $8 million. At the same time, he's about to take his company public and he wants that plant in the corral when he goes public because he thinks he'll make a killing on the public market."

Four weeks later we closed the deal for $13.5 million.

Selling your business doesn't happen every day. It's a once-in-a-lifetime event.

When you make that decision to sell, then you have the power. Whereas if someone else makes that decision for you …

Chapter 26

Fourteen Alternatives to Selling

Some of our clients have come to us because they think selling their business is the only alternative they have. They believe this step to be more like "selling out," or quitting, or jumping ship. They don't want to sell but don't know what else to do.

I would urge you, before you sell your business, to do a rigorous analysis of your business and give serious consideration to your personal future actions.

At Robbinex we perform due diligence on a business before it goes to market. We look at the challenges and current problems, the viability of the business, and long-term opportunities. Some people call that a SWOT (Strengths-Weaknesses-Opportunities-Threats) analysis.

When we tell a business owner they can fix their business, rather than sell it, they often jump at the opportunity. In many cases, they haven't been able to see themselves and their business clearly because they are operating in a Coke bottle. (See chapter 10.)

Here are some alternatives to consider before selling your business:

1 **Refinance** – Find a new bank, or re-mortgage your property, or re-amortize some term loans.

2 **Recapitalize** – Seek out an investor or new financial

partner. Investigate "recaps." This is a new source of financing opportunity. Consider a private placement of an initial public offering.

3 **Burnout** – With all the responsibilities of owning a business you can become so overloaded that you suffer from burnout. A relatively simple solution is available for this situation. Take a break before you break.

4 **Empower the employees** – If this is done well, you have created a management team within the company to help you develop solutions internally. Consider giving long-term employees more authority and responsibility.

5 **Hire a competent manager** – Sometimes the business has grown beyond your ability to manage. Hiring a manager will infuse new skills and support into the business. This will help to solve current challenges and free up your time.

6 **Intergenerational transfer** – Many times your son or daughter would like to be operating the family business but has been unable to communicate effectively with the parent who operates the business. In some cases, they have not had the training that is critical to the success of the business.

7 **Research and planning** – An outside consultant can apply these elements to the business through "new" eyes. Often you have been just too busy to recognize or take advantage of research opportunities and planning.

8 **Miraculous discoveries of value enhancements** – This can happen when you take the time to clearly identify and understand the problems and challenges you are experiencing. These miraculous discoveries can make a huge difference in the life of the business. For example, they can reduce operating costs and increase sales.

9 **Liquidate** – Many times the value of assets is worth more than the value of the business. This is true, for example, of drive-in theatres.

10 **Strategic Alliance** – Create a strategic alliance with some other business to address a particular problem or a project. Such an arrangement can implement the growth of your business and increase profitability.

11 **Amalgamation or merger** – Buy out a competitor, or a near competitor, to obtain additional product lines, customers, employees, capacity, location, etc.

12 **Joint Venture** – In this arrangement two or more similar businesses get together and create a new business to address a common problem or opportunity.

13 **Advisory Boards** – A wonderful and synergistic way to bring many minds together to identify and tackle seemingly insurmountable problems. Interestingly, many members of advisory boards who are viewed as "old guys" have solved problems similar to yours many years ago.

14 **Buy the partner out** – If you are in an unhappy and non-productive partnership, this is often an excellent solution.

Each one of these alternatives can be fairly complex, but you need to think about them before you make a final decision to sell. Selling your business should be your last choice, not your first. Once you have sold it, it's gone. If you realize later that you really shouldn't have sold it, you can't get it back.

Selling may be your best option. But at least consider all the others first.

Chapter *27*

And in Conclusion ...

The purpose of this book has been to give you a view of some of the things that go right and some of the things that go not so right. Selling a business is an exciting time ... and usually one of the most important decisions you will ever make.

Before you need to make a decision about transitioning from your business, whether by selling out or by implementing one of the fourteen alternatives, you need to take the time to *know thyself*. Think about what you will do with the rest of your life. Perhaps you could even get some professional counselling. Be sure to discuss things with your spouse.

Always have a contingency plan in place. I often tell folks that "the day you start your business is the same day you need a plan to exit it." Start with a simple valuation: What is your business really worth? You don't want to go through life with some fantasy value.

Determine when retirement would be ideal for you and your family – and be sure to have some idea of what you would like to do when you retire.

I always like to see long-term planning in most aspects of business operations, and the plan to retire should start five to ten years before your ideal time.

There is much to plan:

- financial planning with your financial planner to ensure you will be financially secure
- business operations (the list here can be quite long)
- tax planning and corporate structuring to minimize taxation
- contingency plans for the business to operate in case of illness (we are more likely to become ill as we grow older)
- power of attorney for the business
- your will
- your power of attorney for your personal effects

With all of these things happening all around us, we have a tendency to make our business lives simple. Interestingly, it often comes down to the Four Levels of Competence.

The first level
Unconscious incompetence: When you don't know what you don't know. Ignorance is bliss.

The second level
Conscious incompetence: When you are conscious of what you don't know. This state can make you feel very insecure and uncomfortable.

The third level
Conscious competence: When you are conscious of what you know. What's interesting about this state is that most often you have to sit down and think things through.

The fourth and final level
Unconscious competence: When you just do things automatically. And everyone around you says, "Man, is this person ever smart." For you it's easy. You don't even have to think about it.

When you move into the unconscious competence state, everything you do seems relatively easy to you. You've spent years moving from being unconsciously incompetent to become conscious of your lack of knowledge to becoming conscious of what you know. And now you just operate on autopilot.

And sometimes you don't realize how much you really know. But this level often leads to complacency, resulting in our failure to be aware of things we don't know or understand because they don't impact our day-to-day lives.

Being unconsciously competent can also be dangerous because you often assume that everybody else around you knows what you know. You may make a lot of assumptions. You may fail to teach. As time passes, you may not take a moment to see what's really happening now. As time passes, elements of business change. You need to get out of your Coke bottle.

If you are an unconsciously competent parent, you need to take a step back one level and work extremely hard to become conscious of your competence. In order for your offspring to successfully follow in your footsteps, you need to teach them what you already know, and you can do that only if you are conscious of your competence.

I speak of this from first-hand experience.

There is so much more to selling a business than just putting up a For Sale sign. If you are that owner who is getting ready to sell a business, you need to have a life plan.

You've got a business plan. You've done your research.

You have looked at your alternatives and said, "You know what? This is what I want to do. My children don't want the business. My employees haven't got the money to buy the business or they haven't got the skills to run it. I don't want to expand and I don't want to amalgamate.

I don't want to bring in a partner. I don't want to hire a manager to run it. So I've looked at all the alternatives. Selling my business is the right decision for me. And now I have to give the intermediary enough time to sell it."

You can come to this conclusion only if you take the time to think things through.

As I have emphasized in this book, there are only two ways to get out of the trench of your business. You can be proactive and build a bridge so you can cross the trench when the time is right for you. Or you can be hauled out of that trench dead or dying.

The choice is yours.

100 SELLER, SELL THYSELF
"Robbins, when are *you* going to sell the business and retire?"

I'm asked that question all the time.

I like what I do and I don't consider that it's work. In fact, my work really is my hobby. I haven't worked since 1974. And I think that's important. Sure we entrepreneurs get stressed, but it's different when it is of our own making as opposed to resulting from working for someone else.

I realize that enjoying my work doesn't mean I won't get sick. It doesn't mean I'm going to live forever. So I have taken my own medicine and have hired people for my team who are twenty years younger than I.

This means in the next four or five years there will be a new breed of people in my company who are ready to come along and continue on. My team and I are putting that infrastructure into place.

I will continue to coach, guide, be the rainmaker, write articles, and attend and speak at conferences.

But I'm going to be here forever ... and don't you forget it!

D.M. (Doug) Robbins

FCBI, M&AMI, CM&A, MCBC, CSBA, CMEA

President and Founder of Robbinex Inc.

Doug started his first business at the age of fourteen, cutting lawns and repairing bicycles. He has since invested in thirty-two businesses. From selling pizza store franchises in 1969 to selling A&W franchises through to 1974, Doug gained valuable insights into the intricacies of selling businesses. He founded Robbinex in 1974 and has worked with thousands of business owners.

Doug's willingness to share his knowledge and experience has resulted in guest appearances in the media, including on CBC's Venture, Citytv News, 680 News, CHCH, CHUM, Bayshore Broadcasting radio programs, and the BNN TV programs Money Talk, SqueezePlay, and Trading Day. He has been featured in the *Financial Post* and *Globe and Mail* newspapers and *Profit* and *Canadian Business* magazines, and has published many articles in a variety of industry magazines.

Doug's keynote presentations have been delivered around the world. His entertaining and educational story-telling presentation style leaves audiences yearning to hear more "Tales from the Trenches."

He may be reached through his website, www.robbinex.com.

CPSIA information can be obtained
at www.ICGtesting.com
Printed in the USA
LVOW04s2122200416

484215LV00028B/123/P